LANCE ARMSTRONG

LANCE ARMSTRONG

John Thompson

Introduction by James Scott Brady,
Trustee, the Center to Prevent Handgun Violence
Vice Chairman, the Brain Injury Foundation

Chelsea House Publishers

Philadelphia

Frontispiece: Lance Armstrong and his Postal Service teammates take a lap of honor in Paris at the conclusion of the 1999 Tour de France.

CHELSEA HOUSE PUBLISHERS

EDITOR IN CHIEF Sally Cheney
ASSOCIATE EDITOR IN CHIEF Kim Shinners
PRODUCTION MANAGER Pamela Loos
ART DIRECTOR Sara Davis
DIRECTOR OF PHOTOGRAPHY Judy L. Hasday

Staff for **Lance Armstrong**
SENIOR EDITOR John Ziff
ASSISTANT EDITOR Rob Quinn
ASSOCIATE ART DIRECTOR/DESIGNER Takeshi Takahashi
PICTURE RESEARCHER Marty Levick
COVER DESIGNER Keith Trego

The Chelsea House World Wide Web address is:
http://www.chelseahouse.com

3 5 7 9 8 6 4 2

Library of Congress Cataloging-in-Publication Data

Thompson, John, 1965-
Lance Armstrong / John Thompson.
  p. cm. — (Overcoming adversity)
Includes bibliographical references and index.

ISBN 0-7910-5879-4 (alk. paper) — ISBN 0-7910-5880-8 (pbk. : alk. paper)

1. Armstrong, Lance—Juvenile literature. 2. Cyclists—United States—Biography
—Juvenile literature. 3. Cancer—Patients—United States—Biography— Juvenile
literature. [1. Armstrong, Lance. 2. Bicyclists. 3. Cancer—Patients.] I. Title.
II. Series.

GV1051.A76 T46 2001
796.6'2'092—dc21
[B]
                                                        00-065972

CONTENTS

OVERCOMING ADVERSITY

TIM ALLEN
comedian/performer

MAYA ANGELOU
author

APOLLO 13 MISSION
astronauts

LANCE ARMSTRONG
professional cyclist

DREW BARRYMORE
actress

JAMES BRADY
gun control activist

DREW CAREY
comedian/performer

JIM CARREY
comedian/performer

BILL CLINTON
U.S. president

TOM CRUISE
actor

GAIL DEVERS
Olympian

MOHANDAS K. GANDHI
political and spiritual leader

MICHAEL J. FOX
actor

WHOOPI GOLDBERG
comedian/performer

EKATERINA GORDEEVA
figure skater

SCOTT HAMILTON
figure skater

JEWEL
singer and poet

JAMES EARL JONES
actor

QUINCY JONES
musician and producer

MARIO LEMIEUX
hockey legend

ABRAHAM LINCOLN
U.S. president

JOHN McCAIN
political leader

WILLIAM PENN
Pennsylvania's founder

JACKIE ROBINSON
baseball legend

ROSEANNE
entertainer

TRIUMPH OF
THE IMAGINATION:
THE STORY OF THE WRITER
J.K. ROWLING
author

MONICA SELES
tennis star

SAMMY SOSA
baseball star

DAVE THOMAS
entrepreneur

SHANIA TWAIN
entertainer

ROBIN WILLIAMS
performer

STEVIE WONDER
entertainer

ON FACING ADVERSITY

James Scott Brady

I GUESS IT'S a long way from a Centralia, Illinois, train yard to the George Washington University Hospital Trauma Unit. My dad was a yardmaster for the old Chicago, Burlington & Quincy Railroad. As a child, I used to get to sit in the engineer's lap and imagine what it was like to drive that train. I guess I always have liked being in the "driver's seat."

Years later, however, my interest turned from driving trains to driving campaigns. In 1979, former Texas governor John Connally hired me as a press secretary in his campaign for the American presidency. We lost the Republican primary to a former Hollywood star named Ronald Reagan. But I managed to jump over to the Reagan campaign. When Reagan was elected in 1980, I was "sitting in the catbird seat," as humorist James Thurber would say—poised to be named presidential press secretary. I held that title throughout the eight years of the Reagan administration. But not without one terrible, extended interruption.

It happened barely two months after the Reagan administration took office. I never even heard the shots. On March 30, 1981, my life went blank in an instant. In an attempt to assassinate President Reagan, John Hinckley Jr. armed himself with a "Saturday night special"—a low-quality, $29 pistol—and shot wildly as our presidential entourage exited a Washington hotel. One of the exploding bullets struck me just above the left eye. It shattered into a couple dozen fragments, some of which penetrated my skull and entered my brain.

The next few months of my life were a nightmare of repeated surgery, broken contact with the outside world, and a variety of medical complications. More than once, I was very close to death.

The next few years were filled with frustrating struggles to function with a paralyzed right side, struggles to speak and communicate.

To people who face and defeat daunting obstacles, "ambition" is not becoming wealthy or famous or winning elections or awards. Words like "ambition" and "achievement" and "success" take on very different meanings. The objective is just to live, to wake up every morning. The goals are not lofty; they are very ordinary.

My own heroes are ordinary folks—but they accomplish extraordinary things because they try. My greatest hero is my wife, Sarah. She's accomplished a lot of things in life, but two stand out. The first has been the way she has cared for me and our son since I was shot. A tremendous tragedy and burden was dropped unexpectedly into her life, totally beyond her control and without justification. She could have given up; instead, she focused her energies on preserving our family and returning our lives to normal as much as possible. Week by week, month by month, year by year, she has not reached for the miraculous, just for the normal. Yet in focusing on the normal, she has helped accomplish the miraculous.

Her other most remarkable accomplishment, to me, has been spearheading the effort to keep guns out of the hands of criminals and children in America. Opponents call her a "gun grabber"; I call her a national hero. And I am not alone.

After a seven-year battle, during which Sarah and I worked tirelessly to educate the public about the need for stronger gun laws, the Brady Bill became law in 1993. It was a victory, achieved in the face of tremendous opposition, that now benefits all Americans. From the time the law took effect through fall 1997, background checks had stopped 173,000 criminals and other high-risk purchasers from buying handguns, and the law has helped to reduce illegal gun trafficking.

Sarah was not pursuing fame, or even recognition. She simply started at one point—when our son, Scott, found a loaded handgun on the seat of a pickup truck and, thinking it was a toy, pointed it at Sarah.

Fortunately, no one was hurt. But seeing a gun nearly bring a second tragedy upon our family, Sarah became determined to do whatever she could to prevent senseless death and injury from guns.

Some people think of Sarah as a powerful political force. To me, she's the person who so many times fed me and helped me dress during my long years of recovery.

Overcoming obstacles is part of life, not just for people who are challenged by disabilities, illnesses, or tragedies, but for all people. No matter what the obstacle—fear, disability, prejudice, grief, or a difficulty that isn't likely to "just go away"—we can all work to make this world a better place.

Lance Armstrong wears the leader's jersey during the ninth stage of the 1999 Tour de France. His victory in the Tour, perhaps the world's most grueling athletic event, capped a miraculous recovery from testicular cancer.

1
TRAINING WHEELS

ON JULY 3, 1999, a 27-year-old American bicycle racer on the U.S. Postal Service team won the opening stage of the Tour de France, a 21-day bicycle race considered by many to be the world's toughest athletic competition. His name was Lance Armstrong, and he was no stranger to pain. Lance would lose the *maillot jaune*—the overall race leader's yellow jersey—during the next week of racing, which took place in the flat farmland of Belgium and western France. This was sprinters' territory, and sprinting was not Lance's forte. But he was a strong rider, and in stage 10, a time trial (a solo race against the clock), he took back the yellow jersey. The following day, the first in the Alps, Lance took a commanding lead, leaving the field of 180 riders far behind and winning the stage. His overall victory was never in doubt from that moment on. Two weeks later, in the final stage, he rode into Paris to become only the second American ever to win the Tour. More importantly for Lance and his many fans, he also became the first cancer survivor to win.

Less than three years earlier, Lance Armstrong had been diagnosed with an advanced case of testicular cancer. Doctors estimated his chance of surviving at below 40 percent. But Lance was a fierce competitor who liked nothing more than a challenge. Drawing upon his deep reserve of strength and courage, he refused to let the cancer beat him. He set about researching the disease and finding the best hospitals and doctors at treating it. He had two goals: first, simply to survive; and second, to resume his racing career. The first depended largely on the mysteries of medical science and luck. The second depended on Lance's heart and courage.

As for those latter qualities, Lance had plenty of both. After all, it seemed he had been fighting against the odds most of his life. His mother, Linda, was only 17 years old when he was born on September 18, 1971, and her husband—a man named Gunderson—left the family around the time Lance turned two. Lance never knew his father and claims to have never even discussed him with his mother. After her husband walked out, Linda, who had worked two jobs while finishing high school, finally got a secretarial position that allowed her to move from Oak Cliff, a dreary, low-income suburb of Dallas, Texas, to a better suburb called Richardson. Soon she got a better job with Ericsson, a large electronics company in the area, and bought a house in the suburb of Plano, just north of Richardson. She also met and married a man named Terry Armstrong.

Though it was a comfort for the family to have two paychecks coming in, Lance never really took to his adoptive father. Terry Armstrong was a born-again Christian who believed that the proper way to bring up a boy was to whip him whenever he was messy, came home late, or generally acted in the rambunctious way young boys sometimes behave. Although his discipline of Lance may never have risen to the level of actual child abuse, it made a firm impression on the boy.

"There was something soul-deadened about the place," Lance said of his hometown of Plano, Texas. Endurance sports became a way to ease the youth's anger and alienation.

But Linda was, and continues to be, a guiding force in Lance's life. When he was young, she worked extra hard to make sure that he always had plenty to eat and that his clothes were clean and pressed. Despite her efforts, there was one thing Linda could not give her son—acceptance from other kids. In Plano, it seemed, being rich or playing football got you noticed. Otherwise people paid little attention to you. As Lance later wrote in his autobiography, *It's Not About the Bike,* "If you weren't a football player you didn't exist, and if you weren't upper middle class, you might as well not exist either." Lance wasn't good at football, and his family certainly wasn't rich.

Luckily, he found a way to channel some of the anger and resentment that even he may not have known was building up inside of him. In the fifth grade he entered and won a distance-running race held at his elementary school. Soon after that, he joined a program at the City of Plano Swim Club. Swimming, although not as big as football, was a popular sport in Plano, and Lance saw it as his chance to fit in. But his first day didn't go as well as he would have liked. Instead of swimming with the kids his own age, he was put with the 7-year-olds based on his lack of skill. It was highly embarrassing for the 12-year-old.

But it was also highly motivating. Remembering his mother's favorite expression, "Make every negative into a positive," Lance decided that if he had to learn to swim with the little kids, then that's just what he'd do. And he'd work twice as hard to get a chance to be with the older kids. He was soon swimming so well that one of the coaches, Chris MacCurdy, took Lance under his wing. Within a year of starting to swim competitively, Lance was placing in the top five at state meets in the 1,500-meter freestyle. Of course, to achieve at this level he went through a tough regimen.

Swim practices were held before and after school. The morning workouts started at 5:30 in the morning! Since it was impossible for Linda to drive Lance to two daily workouts and keep her job, she let him ride his bike. So by the time he was 13, Lance was riding his bike about 20 miles, and swimming an additional 6 miles, each day. As difficult as such a schedule may seem, the high-powered young boy couldn't get enough of it.

It was also about this time that Lance began hanging around a local bike shop, the Richardson Bike Mart. One day he noticed a sign announcing an event called a triathlon. Lance was unfamiliar with this new, grueling competition, but it piqued his interest. It involved swimming, then biking, then running—all in one day. He couldn't believe his eyes. Suddenly there was a sport that involved all three things he was good at. This particular event was a junior triathlon called IronKids that was for

competitors in Lance's age group. He convinced his
mother to let him enter, which wasn't hard. Linda knew
how much sports meant to Lance, and she encouraged him
in every way, especially now that he had found some activ-
ities that held his interest and kept him out of trouble.

His mother scrimped and saved to get Lance a proper
triathlon outfit and his first real racing bike. Even without
time to train adequately, Lance won the event with ease.
Soon he found out about another triathlon in Houston, so
he went down there and again won in a big way. It was as
if a great weight had been lifted from him. Finally, for the
first time in his short life, it didn't matter that he wasn't a
football star or that he didn't have a lot of money. He could
do something that no one else in Plano—or Houston, for
that matter—could do. He could win in one of the most
physically challenging sports open to young athletes. "If it
was a suffer-fest," he later wrote in his autobiography, "I
was good at it."

There was something inside Lance Armstrong that
thrived on the challenge of being a long-distance, multi-
sport athlete, something that allowed him to put his head
down, grit his teeth, and power his way forward to the finish line. He was an angry young man who had a lot of

*At the Richardson Bike Mart,
Lance first heard about
triathlons—races combining
swimming, bicycling, and
running—and he was soon
competing with adults in the
punishing events. Richardson
would also become Lance's
first bike-racing sponsor.*

Sophomore photo of Lance Armstrong from the Plano East High School yearbook. Though an elite athlete, Lance felt like an outsider because he didn't play football and his family wasn't rich.

grudges against the world. He felt like an outsider at school because he didn't play the "right" sports or wear the "right" clothes. His stepfather was cruel and, in Lance's mind, useless. Even when Linda told Lance she was divorcing Terry Armstrong, he had mixed emotions. He was happy that the man who beat him was leaving, but worried that his mother would have to work even harder to keep the family going. And deep down inside, Lance's resentment against his biological father festered like an open wound.

Some of Lance's anger came to the surface in a pretty common way. Like most teenage boys, he had lots of energy and an inventive mind. One time Lance and a friend, Steve Lewis, invented a game they called "fireball." Basically, it was a very dangerous game involving tennis balls that were soaked in kerosene and set on fire. The boys would then put on leather gardening gloves and toss the burning balls back and forth until their gloves began to smoke. Despite once nearly starting a fire when a ball landed on the roof, and watching another ball land in the pan of kerosene and cause an explosion, the boys escaped unharmed.

A few years later, when the boys were old enough to drive, they both had part-time jobs during the Christmas season. Since they worked nights, each was allowed to take the family car to work. They would drag race home at 90 miles per hour down the streets of Plano, tempting fate and creating havoc. Again, they passed through this stage of their lives relatively unscathed.

The majority of Lance's pent-up energy, though, was released through his sport. Focusing on training specifically for the triathlon, Lance entered his first non-junior event, the 1987 President's Triathlon, when he was 15. Although the field was made up of older, more experienced athletes, Lance finished a respectable 32nd—not bad for such a young competitor. In fact, most of the other competitors had doubted whether a 15-year-old could even finish the course, much less perform so well. When a reporter asked him about the race, Lance responded with what would soon become his trademark bravado. "I think in a few years I'll be right near the top," he said. "And within ten years I'll be the best." Most people thought he was just bragging, and even Lance's friends attributed it to his cockiness. But at the President's Triathlon the following year, young Lance finished fifth.

More than simply helping Lance focus his energy, triathlons also helped take care of his material needs. First-place checks were nothing to sneeze at, especially if you were a 15-year-old boy being raised by a single mother. Not only did he enjoy the races, but knowing that he was helping to support the family boosted his confidence. Lance began seeking out triathlons, sometimes even lying about his age in order to be allowed to race. The older athletes, rather than feeling threatened by the youngster, accepted him as one of their own and took to calling him Junior. The unique training and test of endurance the sport involved helped create among its participants a sense of community, a community to which Lance could belong.

Soon Lance began competing in local cycling races in addition to the triathlons. In the world of bicycle racing, each racer is classified according to experience. Everyone starts at Category 4, and the best gradually work their way up to Category 1. The number of races entered, plus the number of those that a rider wins or places highly in, determines the individual ranking. The first races Lance entered as a Cat 4 were called criteriums—multilap races where bonus points are scored for being first across the line on each lap. These races, which have a fast pace from the start, involve lots of high-speed cornering. Because of the number of racers in a "crit," crashes are frequent and tempers can flare. If a rider can make it to the front, he has a better chance of winning a sprint bonus or prime (pronounced "preem"), and a better chance of not being involved in a crash. Lance was generally right at the front, powering past the other Cat 4s with all his might. He was now sponsored by Richardson Bike Mart, so his bike and other equipment were either given to him at no charge or sold at a reduced "pro" price.

The move up the racing ladder from Cat 4 to Cat 1 is a carefully regulated affair. No matter how talented Lance was, it would take a while for him to amass the number of good race finishes needed to be able to compete against older, more experienced guys. There was no doubt he could hold his own in higher crits, but rules were rules. The race promoters had lots of money and their reputations to consider. Letting someone race above his category could cause the other racers to boycott future races or even sue the promoters.

Yet Lance's talent was undeniable. Finally he persuaded the organizers of the Tuesday-night crits to let him race as a Cat 3 even though he hadn't really earned it yet. They allowed Lance to enter the race but told him not to win or there could be trouble. He won it anyway. He was just that much better than the other riders, and his competitive nature wouldn't allow him to lose on purpose. He had been raised by his mother to always do his best no matter what the circumstances—never to quit, back down, or take second to anyone in anything. He had learned her lessons well.

Lance could have been denied his win and even suspended from racing. But the organizers and other racers knew that the problem wasn't Lance, it was the system. Instead of suspending him, they decided to bend the rules and upgrade him. He was now in a position to train and race with a handful of Category 1 riders on the Richardson Bike Mart team. So at the tender age of 16, Lance was beginning to show signs that he was not just a good bike rider, but an amazing athlete who could become a world-class bike racer. He was already making $20,000 a year from his triathlons and local races—enough to buy a Camaro to race around the streets of Plano—and he was quickly making contacts in the bike industry that would help his career along.

All the signs were pointing to success, but Lance was still just a high school kid from Plano, Texas, winning some local races. When he was a junior, however, he traveled to New Mexico for a time trial competition. In these types of races riders start at 30-second to one-minute intervals, and the one with the best time over the course wins. Most time trials are decided by fractions of a second, but Lance was 45 seconds ahead of his closest rival that day. It was just the sort of national attention that he needed. He was invited by the U.S. Cycling Federation—the governing body of professional and amateur cycling in the United States—to train with the junior U.S. national team in Colorado Springs.

The trip to Colorado was only part of the deal. Lance also got to go to Moscow as part of the team to compete in the 1990 Junior World Championships. His first international race, it was a baby step on the road toward his dream of racing in the Tour de France.

Lance crosses the finish line to win the 1993 World Championships in Oslo, Norway. The victory signaled his emergence as a formidable racer in one-day events.

2

THE ROAD
TO SUCCESS

RACING IN THE 1990 Junior World Championships was an eye-opening experience for Lance in two ways. During the race in Moscow, he discovered that his usual approach—going all out from start to finish—wasn't going to be enough for success at the higher levels of competition. That style had won in the Tuesday-night crits and triathlons back in Texas, but in Europe racing was a tactical sport that required discipline and experience. Although Lance had been riding bikes since the age of seven, his European counterparts had been *racing* bikes since that age. However, he was still able to make an impression on the U.S. team officials, as well as a few European team managers, who recognized his raw talent and competitive drive. These are two vital characteristics that just can't be taught.

After returning from Moscow, Lance was shocked to find that the school officials of Plano East High School weren't going to let him graduate. The days he had taken off from school to go to Colorado Springs and Moscow were considered unexcused absences. When the administrators told Lance that he would somehow have to make up the work he had missed, he insisted there was no way he could do it. It was six weeks' worth of work, and he had only a few weeks until graduation. Lance took it especially hard because his mother had already ordered and paid for the graduation announcements and the cap and gown. "I knew damn well if I played football and wore Polo shirts and had parents who belonged to Los Rios Country Club, things would be different," he later wrote in his autobiography.

Lance and his mother refused to give up or give in. Linda called around to every private school in the area until she found one that would allow Lance to transfer his credits and graduate if he agreed to make up some of the work over the summer. He might not have graduated from Plano East High, but Lance Armstrong graduated—on time.

Soon after graduating, Lance got a call from a man named Chris Carmichael, the new director of the U.S. national team. Carmichael was a former Olympian who had once raced with Greg LeMond, an American cycling legend and Lance's hero. Carmichael wanted Lance to join the other team members as they tried to build a successful American cycling program to compete in Europe. The team members included other young cyclists with loads of potential, such as Bobby Julich and George Hincapie. Lance had raced with and against them previously, and he knew they were among the best in the world.

Carmichael was familiar with Lance's reputation for being headstrong and aggressive, but he also saw potential. He knew that Lance's power on the bike and desire to win a race at any cost were rare commodities. Carmichael was confident the skills and tactics of international competition were things Lance could learn. The 1990 World Championships for amateurs, one of Lance's first races as a member of the national team, provided a vivid lesson. Carmichael told Lance to start slow and stay with the pack until the end of the race. "I want you to wait," he said. "I don't want to see you near the front, catching any wind."

Chris Carmichael, director of the U.S. national team, tried to rein in Lance's unbridled aggressiveness and make him a more strategic rider.

It was a 115-mile course with a tough climb at the end. Grabbing an early lead would mean facing the full effects of air drag for a long time, while other riders back in the pack would be able to draft off one another and thus conserve their energy. The smart thing for Lance to do was stay in the *peloton,* or pack of riders, where he could save his strength until the last part of the race. At that point he could break away with an explosive burst and beat the other racers. If Lance made his move too early, though, he would use up all his energy too soon.

Carmichael's strategy was sound, but Lance didn't listen. By the second lap he was already out in front, confident that his strength would be too much for the other

Warming up before a race in his early days riding for the Motorola team, 1992. The brashness of the 21-year-old Texas Bull sometimes grated on European riders.

guys. He was wrong. After a few more laps he was caught by 30 other strong riders, with a lot of racing left to do. He would end up finishing 11th—the best an American had ever done in that race. But it wasn't good enough for Carmichael. Although he was impressed with Lance's power, he was upset with his bullheadedness. "You weren't afraid to fail. You weren't out there thinking, 'What if I got caught?'" Carmichael told his young rider. "Of course, if you had known what you were doing and conserved your energy, you'd have been in the medals." But one lesson wouldn't be enough for the racer dubbed the Texas Bull.

Lance eventually captured his first two major wins in 1992 at the First Union Grand Prix in Atlanta and the Thrift Drug Classic in Pittsburgh. That same year he helped represent the United States at the Olympic Games held in Barcelona, Spain, where he placed 14th in the road race.

Immediately after the Olympics he entered his first European race as a professional. It was the San Sebastián Classic, which was also held in Spain. The classics are hard, long, one-day races. Lance would dominate this sort of racing later in his career, but in his pro debut, in a cold, driving rainstorm, he finished dead last. As he plowed ahead to the finish line, nearly 30 minutes behind the winner, the crowd laughed at him. The experience was so humiliating that Lance flirted with the idea of giving up professional cycling entirely. The important thing, though, was that he had finished the race. Fifty other riders had dropped out, but Lance just gritted his teeth and kept turning his pedals. Two weeks later, in Zurich, Switzerland, Lance took second place in a World Cup race.

In the months ahead, Lance Armstrong began to make his mark on the staid world of international cycling—but not necessarily in a positive way. "I raced with no respect. Absolutely none," he confessed. "I paraded, mouthed off, shoved my fists in the air." He began to make enemies among the European riders. He was, by his own admission, "still the kid from Plano with a chip on my shoulder, riding headlong, pedaling out of anger."

But Lance really started to show where his talent and drive could take him in 1993. He won the Thrift Drug Triple Crown by winning the Thrift Drug Classic, K-Mart Classic, and CoreStates. Then he won the U.S. National Pro Road Race. He also won a stage in each the Tour DuPont, Tour of Sweden, and Tour of America Race Series.

Racing in Europe for a U.S. team sponsored by Motorola, Lance took his first crack at the Tour de France in 1993. He had already proved he could do well in one-day events, and he had finished second in the Tour DuPont, a stage race along the East Coast of the United States. More importantly, he had shown that he could lead his team in a long stage race, something not many 21-year-old first-year pros even get a chance to do. But the Tour de France is different. It's the Super Bowl, the World Series, and the Stanley Cup all rolled into one and spread over more than two weeks. It's both beautiful and brutal in its extremes. "You have to be seasoned for the Tour," says Jim Ochowicz, former Motorola general manager and still one of Armstrong's biggest supporters. "The Tour takes victims, during the race and after. You can be out for a month, for a year after the Tour. You don't just go and win it. It's a process of testing limits, learning. That is what Lance [had] to do. He [had] to get the miles."

In his initial crack at the Tour de France, Lance raced in the first 11 stages of the 21-day event. (The Tour can be from 21 to 23 days long, depending on the route chosen by the promoters, the Société du Tour de France.) Young, aggressive riders often have plenty of chances to win a stage or two in the first week to 10 days. The older riders who feel they have a chance of finishing on the podium in Paris know that the real racing doesn't start until the riders reach the Pyrenees and then the Alps, the two mountain ranges bordering France. As one of those young, aggressive riders, Lance won the eighth stage, then dropped out a few days later in 62nd place. But he got the miles.

A month later on the rain-slick streets of Oslo, Norway, Lance Armstrong had the race of his young life. It was the 1993 World Championships, a one-day race that would determine who would get to wear the rainbow stripes of the world champion on his jersey for the next year. Because of the rain, speeds were slow and there were many crashes. Lance himself crashed at one point. But by the final lap of the course he was at the front of the pack along with Miguel Indurain, the reigning Tour de France champion and the favorite to win the Worlds. On the last climb, Lance attacked and caught his rivals napping. Not only were they not looking for an attack in such horrible conditions, but they sure weren't looking for it from some upstart American. There was no way for the rest of the field to answer the attack, so Lance cruised across the finish line, his arms raised in a brash, all-American victory salute. He then put his own stamp on the event by inviting his mother, Linda, to join him on the victor's podium— simply another unexpected jolt he would give to the conservative world of professional bicycle racing.

If Lance's career can be split into two distinct periods—

pre- and postcancer—then the 1993 World Championships in Oslo could be called the defining moment of the first period. "This day changed my life," he says. "The expectation levels grew. I can look back now and see levels that I have hit, and I know there are other levels ahead." Lance continued working hard to reach those next levels by racing in both Europe and the United States in 1994. He got a stage win and second place in the Tour DuPont, and he continued to excel in the one-day races. His aggressive riding style and muscular build lent themselves to the one-day races. In the longer, multiday stage races, he could maybe win a stage or two but would invariably run out of gas before it was all over.

The next year, 1995, would be another landmark year in Lance Armstrong's cycling career. First, in the spring, he accomplished a goal that had been just out of his reach for the previous two years. The biggest race in America was the Tour DuPont, which began in Wilmington, Delaware, and after 12 days of racing ended in Greensboro, North Carolina. It wasn't the Tour de France by any means, but it attracted some of the big-name Europeans, such as Russian star Viatcheslav Ekimov and Swiss sensation Tony Rominger, one of the best bicycle racers in the world at the time. Lance had come in second to Ekimov in 1994 and was determined not to do so again. At the prologue in Wilmington he put it in plain words: "I don't want to finish second again." A few days later in Asheville, North Carolina, he made it even plainer: "I don't think you should have to have 10 interpreters to interview the winner of the race." For Lance, there was much more at stake than simply adding another win to his résumé. Victory in this race was a matter of national pride.

Winning a stage race, though, was not going to be easy for Lance. Although he was an accomplished one-day racer—he could win the grueling one-day races in Europe and the United States by sheer force—his weakness was the multiday stage races, such as the Tour DuPont. But if he were ever to have a chance at winning the Tour de France, he would need to win this race. Lance had lost the previous year's Tour DuPont in the time trials.

The ironic thing was that when Lance first began racing as a professional, time trials were one of his better skills. Mountains had been his weakness. Coming from Texas, he hadn't had much of a chance to practice riding up the steep slopes that he would one day face in Europe or even in America's Tour DuPont, which went through the Smoky Mountains. Also, because of his years as a swimmer and triathlete, Lance had a bigger upper-body build than most cyclists—muscles in his chest and arms had been pumped up by all those laps in the Plano Swim Club pool. More body weight meant a tougher time pedaling uphill.

The only way to get better at climbing was to climb. Lance practiced in the Rocky Mountains and in the Alps of Europe. But that meant he wasn't working as much on his time trials. In bicycle racing a rider must have several skills. He must be able to climb in the mountains, race against the clock in the time trial, and sprint for bonus points or a finish line.

Yet some racers concentrate on only one skill. Italy's Marco Cipollini and Belgium's Tom Steels are pure sprinters. They have huge thighs and broad shoulders. They aren't afraid of bumping into other riders at 45 miles per hour in a bunch sprint at the end of a race. But they usually stay away from any race with mountains. Then there are the time trialers, such as England's Chris Boardman. Tall and thin, these racers aren't so good in packs and prefer to test their endurance and pain threshold against the clock. Most aren't too good in the mountains either. Finally, there are the climbers, such as France's Richard Virenque and Italy's Marco Pantani. Thin, light, and small, these racers don't have the muscle mass to contest a sprint or beat the clock, but in the mountains they put distance between themselves and the competition.

The riders who win stage races such as the Tour de France and Tour DuPont are known as all-around racers. They may not excel in any one skill, but they are good enough at each to make a crucial difference in the race. Such competitors may not sprint as well as a Cipollini, but they sprint better than the other guys when it matters. They may not be pure climbers like a Pantani, but they are good enough to stay at the front during the mountain stages. Greg LeMond, Eddy Merckx, Bernard Hinault, and Miguel Indurain are four of the greatest all-around riders of the last 30 years. If Lance wanted to win the 1995 Tour DuPont, and by extension to ever have a shot at a Tour de France title, he needed to become an all-around rider.

After Lance's second-place finish to Ekimov in the 1994 Tour DuPont, he and his coaches realized that he needed to improve his time trials, while not sacrificing his climbing ability. During the off-season Lance worked hard at perfecting his position on the bike. He spent many hours on a stationary bike in a wind tunnel, hooked up to a computer that analyzed his aerodynamic position. The purpose of this type of work is to minimize the amount of wind resistance a rider faces. Lance also experimented with his seat height and focused on improving his attitude toward time trials. Rather than hate them, he retrained his brain so that he actually looked forward to them. It's this sort of dedication to a sport that pushes one athlete above the crowd into greatness. And it paid off big time for Lance.

The 4th stage of the 12-stage Tour DuPont race took the riders across four mountains in the state of Virginia on the way from Lynchburg to Blacksburg. On the third mountain Lance left Ekimov behind and won the stage by more than two minutes. The next day was a time trial, and Lance's training paid off again. He beat Ekimov to win the stage. He stayed in the lead for the rest of the race, putting even

Lance celebrates his 1995 Tour DuPont victory, his first stage-race win. The patriotic young Texan was particularly proud that his triumph had come on American soil.

more time between himself and Ekimov on the long climb up North Carolina's Beech Mountain in stage 10. By the time the race moved to the final stage, Lance was more than four minutes ahead of Ekimov, who was in third place.

The last stage, however, was a time trial. But this time, with his lead, Lance knew that unless he crashed and hurt himself, he would end up the winner. "I'll be conservative," he said before the race. "I'll go all out on the flat stretches, but I'll back off on the turns." The effects of winning in the mountains and the previous time trial showed, as Lance's form was off and he was visibly stiff. But true to his word, he rode just fast enough to keep his lead, conceding the stage win to Ekimov but keeping the race leader's yellow jersey and the right to call himself the overall winner.

It was more than just an American winning an American race, although that was news enough. The inaugural race had been held in 1989, and only one other American had ever won the overall: the great Greg LeMond, who was also the only American ever to win the Tour de France. "It's as big as anything I've ever won," said Lance at his victory celebration. "I won the world championship two years ago, but that was a one-day race. This was over a number of days. And this was here."

On the eve of his third Tour de France, Lance was no less intense but considerably more mature. "I think I have a better understanding of the Tour de France now and how grand it is," he told reporters.

3

GETTING
THE MILES

IN JULY OF 1995, 23-year-old Lance Armstrong lined up to start his third Tour de France. He was hopeful in a way that suggested he was beginning to grow out of being the boastful, aggressive young Texan. "I'm definitely fit, much more fit than I've ever been in my life, ever," said Lance just before the start. "I think I have a better understanding of the Tour de France now and how grand it is and what it truly means to the sport and to the sponsors and the people." His newfound maturity was brought about by a combination of things. First, he had been somewhat humbled in 1994—a year in which he didn't win a single race all season. After his much ballyhooed entrance into professional cycling, he hadn't done much more than shoot off his mouth. But he had learned a lot from that experience, and some of it didn't have as much to do with racing bikes as it did with becoming a better person.

Thanks to hard work and dedication during the off-season, Lance had started 1995 on a very positive note. He had won several major races in the United States, including the 12-stage Tour DuPont, the

biggest race in America. Then he had done well in the Tour
of Switzerland. Even more important, though, was that
another year had passed and he felt himself growing
stronger, both physically and mentally. "I expect that
progress," he candidly told a group of reporters before the
Tour de France got under way. "Just as I expect a year
from now I'll be stronger than I am now. I'm only 23 years
old. I fully expect to have steps like that for the next five
years. That's reasonable, that's natural and normal." But
just because he was a bit more mature didn't mean the
Texas Bull was becoming the Texas Bore. Going through
the maps of all the stages with reporters, Lance confi-
dently showed off the profiles of the stages he expected to
win. He showed a profile of the 13th stage. "It'll be hot
and I like that," he said, "and all these ups and downs, I
like that."

No matter how strong he felt or how much confidence
he displayed in the interviews before the racing began,
Lance's chances of winning the Tour that year were actually pretty slim. It could happen, of course—anything was
possible. But even Lance knew that the best he could hope
for was to finish in the top 10, if he could finish at all. Lots
of strong riders abandon the 2,300-odd-mile Tour de
France every year. Some crash out, some develop a cold
they can't get over, and some just feel they can't finish. It's
that hard.

Lance also knew that he was going up against the best
riders in the world, including the reigning Tour champion
from Spain, Miguel Indurain. Big Mig, as he was called,
was the undisputed boss of the Tour—in the lingo of the
European racing scene, he was called the *patrón*. Not only
did he call the shots for his own team, but he also served
as a sort of informal representative of the riders. Although
disputes between riders and the Tour's organizers were
rare, they did occasionally arise. One example was the
attempt in the early 1990s by the Société du Tour de
France to force the riders to wear helmets at all times. The

riders, most of whom had grown up in Europe not wearing helmets, protested and threatened to strike. The Tour organizers backed down quickly.

Unfortunately, the 1995 Tour would require Big Mig to step into his roll of *patrón*—and underscore the validity of a helmet rule. The Tour that year would also bring Lance Armstrong and his Motorola teammates face-to-face with their own mortality.

It happened in the 15th stage, on July 18, 1995. The riders were in the Pyrenees of southern France, on the border with Spain. Motorola team rider Fabio Casartelli, along with a few other riders, crashed on the steep, windy decline leading down from the Portet d'Aspet pass, the first of six climbs for that day. Casartelli skidded across the pavement and into a curb on the outside of the turn. He was not wearing a helmet. He fractured his skull, and on the emergency helicopter flight to a nearby hospital in Tarbes, France, he died of coronary failure. His heart stopped from loss of blood and shock. The doctors couldn't revive him. He became the third racer to die during the Tour since it began in 1903.

Although he had raced for the Motorola team, which was based in the United States, Fabio Casartelli had been a rising Italian superstar. He had won the gold medal in the 1992 Olympics in Barcelona and was only two years older than Lance Armstrong. He left behind a young wife and a four-month-old son. The news didn't reach the rest of the team until after the stage was over. Shocked, they were all unsure if they wanted to finish the race. "Personally, I wanted to stop," Lance later wrote. "I simply didn't think I had the heart to ride a bike. It was the first time I had encountered death, and genuine grief, and I didn't know how to handle it. But then Fabio's wife came to see us, and she said she wanted us to keep riding, because she felt that was what Fabio would have wanted. So we sat in the grass behind the hotel, said a few prayers, and decided to stay in."

This page: Motorola rider
Fabio Casartelli, who died
after a crash during the 15th
stage of the 1995 Tour de
France. Opposite page:
Pointing heavenward, Lance
dedicates his stage-18 win to
his fallen friend.

The next morning, the *peloton* gathered at the start line for a moment of silence in honor of their fallen comrade. There wasn't any friendly boasting or trash talking on this day. Instead the faces of the cyclists were marked by the emotions they felt. Each one knew that his job was to push himself to the very limits of human endurance to win. It was a dangerous job, but these men pursued it with bravery and skill. Casartelli had been one of them, a brother-in-arms. The leader of the Tour, Miguel Indurain, with the consent of all 118 riders still left in the race, declared that there would be no racing that day. Instead they rode in

procession along the course to honor Casartelli. The Motorola team was allowed to ride in the front of the group. When the *peloton* reached the finish line, Motorola rider Andrea Peron, an Italian, was allowed to cross first, taking the stage in Fabio Casartelli's name.

Two days later, during the 18th stage, a route from Bordeaux to Limoges, Lance Armstrong gave his friend Casartelli a tribute in his own style. In 1995 the Tour was only 20 stages long. Lance and the other riders knew that if they were to have a chance to win the whole thing, or at the very least move up in the rankings, it would have to come in this stage. Lance also knew that Fabio Casartelli had set his sights on winning the stage into Limoges. Although they were out of the mountains, there were still a few smaller climbs to get over. Lance was among a group of 12 cyclists who had broken away from the main pack and had built up a small but important lead. On the last climb, the impetuous Texan dug deep into his soul and launched an attack that caught the other riders off guard. They were probably thinking about how glad they were that the mountains were truly done or how they would try to place themselves in the final sprint only 30 kilometers away. Whatever the case, they clearly were not ready for an attack.

Lance, however, knew that his strength wasn't in a bunch sprint, but in his ability to push himself harder than anyone else. Because his jump took the other riders by surprise and they were all on different teams, they couldn't get themselves organized to respond. Having put all of his emotion, energy, and strength into his surprise attack, Lance looked back with one kilometer to go and saw that he was free and clear. As he approached the finish line, he sat up straight, pointed to the heavens, and dedicated his win to his friend and former teammate Fabio Casartelli. This display of emotion endeared Lance to the Italian race fans. "Certainly I learned more about life and death in this

Tour than I learned about bike racing," said Lance. "More than anything else, I learned how to deal with death."

But Lance also admitted that he had grown as a bike racer just by finishing the Tour. "There were no shortcuts, I realized," he wrote in his autobiography. "It took years of racing to build up the mind and body and character, until a racer had logged hundreds of races and thousands of miles of road. I wouldn't be able to win a Tour de France until I had enough iron in my legs, and brain, and heart. Until I was a man. Fabio had been a man. I was still trying to get there."

He had learned a lot about becoming a man in the summer of 1995. But it wouldn't be long before he would understand just how much more there was to learn.

The cycling world expected 1996 to be a breakout year for Lance Armstrong. Instead, it would be a season of subpar performances—and the reason wouldn't become known until late in the year.

4

A BUMPY ROAD

OVER THE WINTER of 1995–96, Lance dedicated himself to working even harder than usual to prepare for what he hoped would be the best season of his career. After his successes at the end of the previous summer, it was widely believed in the cycling world that 1996 was to be the Year of Lance.

Yet the 1996 season started out with Lance trying to recover his fitness after a crash in an early-spring race in Spain. Because he was forced to spend a week off the bike, his spring races, and indeed the whole season, were suddenly in jeopardy. For amateur weekend warriors a week off the bike can actually improve performance, as it allows the body time to recuperate. But for racers at Lance's level it can be a major setback that takes months to get over. Professionals are always riding, even in the off-season; on what are called "rest" days, they're still out on the bike, putting miles into their legs. These athletes race into top form, using the stress of competition to hone their bodies into hardened machines of flesh and blood.

Despite his off-season preparation, the accident had Lance struggling for second-place finishes in races he had anticipated winning. He received a second blow in May of 1996, when the Motorola Corporation announced that it was withdrawing its sponsorship of an international race team at the end of the season. As in professional car racing and other motor sports, professional bicycle race teams have corporate sponsors who basically use the team as a form of advertising. When Lance won a race, Motorola got lots of attention, since its name was plastered all over his jersey and shorts. But sometimes a corporation decides that its advertising dollars can be better spent on something other than supporting a racing team.

Losing sponsorship isn't the end of the road for bicycle racers, since most of them spend the off-season negotiating new deals with current or prospective sponsors anyway. But losing the backing of a sponsor based in the United States was a little demoralizing to Lance, who was proud to be an American winning in Europe for an American team. At the same time, though, needing to impress prospective new teams forced Lance to kick-start his racing after the early-season slump. He was used to pulling down nearly $750,000 a year and was ranked seventh in the world, so he needed to keep his winning streak alive if he wanted a good contract for the following year. "I had a feeling Motorola wouldn't return," said Lance. "So to have to go out and maybe find a new team, find a new contract, find a new salary, I had to be super."

And of course he was super. Being under that sort of pressure only brought out the best in Lance—and his teammates. Crediting part of their success to the memory of their fallen comrade in the previous year's Tour, the Motorola boys dominated the European spring classics, such as Paris-Nice and Liège-Bastogne-Liège, as well as the Tour DuPont in America, which Lance won for the second year in a row. Consummate professionals, the team pulled together to win, even as each rider actively sought out another team for the upcoming season. All the while Jim Ochowicz, Motorola's *director sportif*—the term for the coach in professional bicycle racing—sought a new sponsor for the old team. If Ochowicz could find another company to take over for Motorola, he could keep his winning combination of riders together. But it wasn't easy finding a corporation to come up with the millions of dollars needed to support a professional team. Ochowicz told his riders that if he didn't have a new sponsor by July, they were free to find other employment.

The pressure of getting a spot on a team for the next season made preparing for the Tour de France even harder than usual. Lance had taken a few weeks off in May to get settled in a new house he had purchased in Austin, Texas. There he began fielding calls from various European teams—a not unusual situation in the cycling world. Teams are eager to have the best talent and are always courting racers of Lance's ability. But his year was different because of Motorola's announcement. Although some American-based teams wanted to hire him, Lance had a specific goal in mind. "I have goals in this sport that I would like to achieve," he said. "I could go with Saturn or Postal Service, an American team, but I would not achieve my goals with them. I realize I have to go somewhere European."

As the Tour de France approached, Lance and the rest of the Motorola team knew that their performances in the race could be the difference between getting a spot on one of the best teams, getting a spot on any team, or heading home to sit out the next season. But as the race got under way, there was another consideration: the Olympic road race. Scheduled just 10 days after the end of the Tour, the race was important to Lance for two reasons. First, it was the Olympics. Although the Tour may be the biggest race in the world, the Olympics are coveted because they only come around every four years. The great Miguel Indurain ended up winning five Tours de France in a row, but to win even one Olympic race was outside his ability. The second reason was one that had always motivated the patriotic Texan. The 1996 Olympics were being held in Atlanta, Georgia, and Lance believed that only an American should win on American soil. He also knew that Americans were more likely to watch a one-day Olympic race than they were to sit through the three weeks of foreign names and places of the Tour de France.

There was another reason the 1996 Olympics were so important to Lance and the rest of the world's professional racers. For the first time, the race would be open to professionals, not just amateurs. The 1992 Olympic road race had been Lance's last event as an amateur. He turned pro immediately after the race. Four years later he was getting the chance to go for the gold again—a feather in his cap that he had missed the last time.

Although he was ranked fourth in the world at the time the Tour began, he quickly fell five minutes behind the leader by the fifth stage. Saying that he was looking ahead to the race in Atlanta and the fall World Cup races, Lance put his physical condition at only about 75 percent of what it could be. Attributing it to a nearly month-long layoff between the Tour DuPont and the Tour de France, Lance let everyone know that he was not slacking off, but instead riding tactically in preparation for Atlanta.

But in the sixth stage of the 1996 Tour de France, Lance pulled to the side of the road, ripped off his race number, and officially took himself out of the race. It had been raining for days, and Lance wasn't the only one to bow out on that day. It wasn't unusual for a rider to catch a cold and pull out of a race as tough as the Tour, and that's all Lance figured was wrong with him. "I couldn't breathe," he said. "I started feeling a little sick last night. I'm bummed, but if I'm sick, I'm sick, and I have to stop." Lance had now dropped out of three of the four Tours de France he had entered, and had seriously shortened his preparation for the Olympic race.

*Lance bears down during
the Olympic road race,
August 3, 1996. Though
he'd hoped to win a medal
at the Atlanta Games, he
finished in 12th place, well
out of contention.*

After Lance left the Tour, his primary concern was his friend Jim Ochowicz's inability to find a replacement sponsor for the team. Although some companies had made initial offers, Ochowicz hadn't been able to get anyone to sign on the dotted line. With Lance out of the Tour and not overly confident of an Olympic medal, Ochowicz was finding it even harder to land a new sponsor. Likewise, Lance was finding it hard to lock in a contract should

*Racing coach Jim Ochowicz
scrambled to find a new
sponsor for his riders
after Motorola announced
its decision to withdraw
sponsorship at the conclusion
of the 1996 season. Despite
Ochowicz's efforts, the
talented American-based
team was broken up, and
Lance signed with the French
Cofidis organization.*

Ochowicz fail to come through for the team. Festina, a powerful French team, had made verbal offers but withdrew them after Lance dropped out of the Tour. "That's okay. They'll realize their mistake soon enough," said an obviously bitter Lance.

In the much anticipated Olympic race, Lance finished a disappointing 12th place. He remarked that the racecourse didn't suit him—it was mainly flat with only one small climb. Lance simply wasn't able to generate the power he needed to break away from the group. Putting it down to his lack of adequate training, the poorly designed course, and the heat and humidity of Atlanta, Lance didn't spend much time worrying about the race. He became more concerned with the fall World Cup schedule and signing a contract with a new team.

Lance finally signed a contract with the French-based Cofidis team—a brand-new team just forming for the 1997 season—for a remarkable $1.25 million over two years. Joining Lance on the team would be his Motorola buddies Frankie Andreu and Bobby Julich, and guiding it all would be the world-famous cycling coach Cyrille Guimard, the man responsible for launching Greg LeMond's fabulous career. Despite this welcome news, Lance's racing in the final half of the 1996 season was less than spectacular. He was still good, of course, but not great. His plans to win the World Cup were put on hold in September, with two months left in the season. His 12th-place finish in the Olympic road race, along with the mediocre results in the San Sebastián Classic, Leeds International, and other fall races, convinced Lance that he needed to return to Austin to rest. It was the gut reaction of an athlete, but it would turn out to be a lifesaving decision.

Before the diagnosis, 1996. Determination and toughness developed over a lifetime of overcoming obstacles would serve Lance well in his coming battle with cancer.

5

AN UNEXPECTED DETOUR

PROFESSIONAL ATHLETES ARE different from the typical weekend warrior. It's not just that they can jump higher, run farther, or swim faster. It's that they have the mental discipline and the physical ability to push their bodies harder than most of us. Generally, spectators see only the game-day heroics, the adoration of fans, and the big-money endorsement deals that athletes receive. What isn't seen are the hours upon hours of training that these men and women put themselves through, sometimes for nothing more than the right to call themselves the fastest or the strongest.

In many respects, professional bicycle racing is one of the hardest, most physically challenging sports around. Because riding a bike is a nonimpact activity, however, a racer really has no reason not to ride every day. Unlike running or weight lifting, riding a bike is not that physically stressing on the body's joints. For this reason, the racers can push themselves to extreme speeds and distances that tax other aspects of the body and mind. Although 100-mile footraces are not unheard of in this age of extreme sports, it's unlikely we'll ever see a footrace to equal the Tour de France. One rider likened the Tour to hitting his thighs with hammers for two weeks straight. The risk of injury is great, as racing in the Alps and Pyrenees eventually takes its toll. Racers like Lance Armstrong learn to do more than merely live with pain; they learn to use it to their advantage by taking more of it than the next guy can. They are constantly pushing themselves harder, faster, and farther than their opponents.

It's difficult to tell if this ability to absorb more pain than the next guy is physical, mental, or a little of both. Lance claims that he discovered his ability to suffer more than most at a young age. Part of it had to do with his upbringing. The only son of a very young single mother, Lance was not brought up to be a whiner. His mother, Linda, once told him, "Look, Lance, if you're going to get anywhere, you're going to have to do it yourself, because no one is going to do it for you." In school he was looked down on by some of the wealthy kids because he didn't wear the "right" clothes or belong to the "right" clubs or play the "right" sports. All of this, plus the fact that he didn't know his father, caused the young man a lot of emotional pain.

But he learned to use that pain to his benefit. Emotional pain and anger fueled his competitive drive. In turn, Lance says, distance running or riding a bike fast helped ease the pain that was in his heart. Along the way he discovered something else: he had an extraordinary ability to withstand *physical* pain as well. When it came to going long distances, testing his endurance—dealing with that sort of pain—he could beat anyone. Unsuccessful at football and other ball sports, Lance first found his niche in running and swimming before discovering bike riding. He eventually put the three together to become a champion triathlete while still in high school. As his professional cycling career took off, and his winning record increased, it was this ability to overcome pain that led him to still greater achievements. His success in the brutal one-day races in Europe was born of his ability to endure pain. And his transformation from one-day racer to multistage racer was also due to his ability to go past the pain.

But his natural tendency to endure pain without complaint almost cost him his life.

Lance probably should have known something was wrong way back in the spring of 1996, after winning the Tour DuPont. Instead of being hyped about winning the race for the second time in a row, he was exhausted. He simply crossed the finish line—no two-fisted salute, no hand pumping, nothing. And although he dropped out of the Tour de France later that summer because of a cold and a steady dose of rainy, dismal weather, looking back, the signs were there that something else was wrong with him. Young, strong professional racers don't drop out of a race just because of a little damp weather. Despite the fact that he performed reasonably well at the Olympics and in some of the fall races, there was no doubt he should have done better. Something was wrong, but his ability to withstand pain didn't let him notice it.

Lance had noticed a swelling of his right testicle, and then one night in late September of 1996 he coughed up blood while talking to a friend on the telephone. Suddenly the pain was not something simply to be ignored. This seemed serious. So Lance called his friend and neighbor Dr. Rick Parker, who also happened to be his personal physician when at home in Austin. Dr. Parker checked Lance's throat and thought it might simply be a cracked sinus caused by Lance's allergies. But then Lance told him about his sore testicle. Dr. Parker told Lance to immediately see one of the most prominent urologists (a doctor who treats urinary and genital problems) in Austin. Dr. Parker even made the appointment with Dr. Jim Reeves for Lance. Dr. Parker knew that Lance should be checked out, but he really didn't have any inkling as to the seriousness of Lance's condition. He suspected that the swollen testicle was perhaps cycling related, and that all Lance would need was rest.

The appointment with Dr. Reeves was, in Lance's mind, almost unnecessary. Like a lot of men, especially young men, Lance wasn't comfortable going to see a doctor, even for something as potentially serious as a swollen testicle. Dr. Reeves, however, took one look at Lance's swollen testicle and ordered an ultrasound and chest X rays. The "routine" examination was suddenly not so routine. Even Lance, fearless as a bicycle racer, was nervous and confused. Later that evening, sitting across from Dr. Reeves, Lance was given a diagnosis that strikes fear in the heart of all who receive it. He had cancer.

"I thought I knew what fear was, until I heard the words *You have cancer*," he later wrote in his autobiography. "Real fear came with an unmistakable sensation: it was as though my blood started flowing in the wrong direction. My previous fears, fear of not being liked, fear of being laughed at, fear of losing my money, suddenly seemed like cowardice. Everything now stacked up differently: the anxieties of life . . . were reprioritized into need versus want, real problem as opposed to minor scare."

Affecting nearly 7,000 men a year in the United States, testicular cancer is a disease that mostly strikes young men between the ages of 18 and 25. It's a treatable type of cancer with a high rate of cure if it's caught early enough. But Lance hadn't listened when his body tried to tell him something was wrong. Familiar with pain, he had ignored the warning signs so long that his cancer had spread into his abdomen and lungs. For months Lance had felt tired, experienced terrible headaches, and suffered with pain. Recently his vision had become blurred. Now he was faced with a challenge tougher than any opponent he had ever raced against. But it wasn't a yellow jersey he was competing for now—it was his life.

Although Dr. Reeves was confident of his diagnosis, he didn't know the extent to which the cancer had spread. The

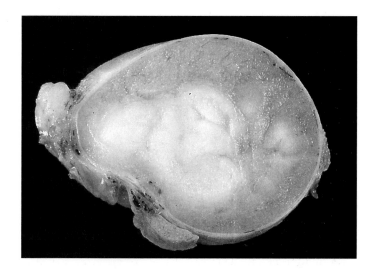

The lighter section at the center of this photo of a human testicle is a malignant tumor called a seminoma. Testicular cancer, which strikes mostly men between the ages of 18 and 25, is highly treatable if caught early—but very deadly otherwise.

first step, however, was to remove the cancerous testicle as quickly as possible. Dr. Reeves scheduled Lance for surgery for the following day.

Although his very life hung in the balance, Lance admits that at this point, he was still more concerned with not being able to race. When he got home that night, Lance called his agent, Bill Stapleton. "Bill, I have some really bad news," he said. "I'm sick, I'm never going to race again, and I'm going to lose everything." Then he hung up.

He had worked hard for everything he ever had in life. While most people his age were learning a skill or trade, or working toward a college degree, Lance had been learning how to beat the best cyclists in the world. It was a good living and he loved it. It made him something bigger than the unpopular kid from Plano who couldn't afford Polo shirts or play football. Now that it was all at risk, Lance was starting to learn that maybe there was more to him than merely being a guy who could ride a bike fast.

That night Lance finally had a chance to think. The aura of invincibility cultivated by most athletes—and *for* most athletes by those around them—evaporated. "As I sat in my house alone that first night," he wrote, "it was humbling to be so scared. More than that, it was humanizing."

The next few days would be hectic for Lance and his family and friends. The first step was the surgery to remove the affected testicle. It was a fairly routine procedure, with an almost certain outcome. Everything went great, but the results of the accompanying biopsy were less than comforting. According to the tests, the cancer was spreading rapidly. This is one of the worst characteristics of testicular cancer: if caught early enough, it is little more than an inconvenience; otherwise, it can spread quickly through the lymph system into the abdomen, the lungs, and even the brain. Because of the X rays, Lance already knew it had spread to his lungs, but he and his doctors hoped it had gone no farther.

The next step in Lance's treatment would be the dreaded chemotherapy. The idea behind chemo, as it's called, is to introduce a highly poisonous substance into the body in a controlled fashion. The poison kills the cancerous cells. Of course, healthy cells can be killed too. The result is almost always a series of terrible side effects for the patient, which include nausea, susceptibility to other illnesses, and hair loss. Even worse for Lance was the fact that the combination of the surgery plus the chemo would almost certainly make it impossible for him ever to become a father. Despite his focus on bike racing, Lance had always wanted to be the kind of father he'd never had. To make sure he could one day fulfill his dream of being a dad, Lance would have to visit a sperm bank in the nearby city of San Antonio.

The week before he was to start chemo, however, he got a call from Dr. Dudley Youman, the Austin-based oncologist who had taken over Lance's case from Dr. Reeves. Dr. Youman, considered one of the finest oncologists in Austin, was interested in treating Lance as aggressively as possible. The news Dr. Youman had for Lance was not good. The cancer was spreading even more rapidly than the initial tests had indicated. The blood counts used to track the disease were showing high levels of certain types

of proteins that indicate the speed of the cancer's progression through the body. Lance's protein levels had risen sharply in just one day, an indication that he needed to begin the chemo sooner than expected. In fact, Dr. Youman wanted to begin the chemo the following day, which meant that Lance had to rush down to the San Antonio sperm bank that very day to make sure he wouldn't miss his chance at fatherhood.

Deep inside Lance Armstrong a cancer was growing. But that wasn't all. A stronger sense of the future and of his place in the world, along with a recognition that there was more to life than riding a bike, was also beginning to grow within his heart.

The sickness was beginning to shape Lance in a way that he could never have imagined. As a young man, and even while a pro bicycle racer, he had never really turned his thoughts inward. Instead he looked out at the world

Dr. Lawrence Einhorn (left) and Lance Armstrong testify at Senate hearings on biotechnology funding. Einhorn pioneered the treatment for testicular cancer that would ultimately save Lance's life.

and challenged it on a daily basis. He had worked hard and sweat buckets to get where he was, and though not easy, it had seemed effortless. As a kid he got on a bike and rode faster than anyone else, and this talent eventually brought him money and fame. It had bought him a million-dollar home and a Porsche. What it couldn't bring him, though, was self-knowledge.

From the moment he found out he was sick, Lance had been obsessed with his racing career and the thought that it might all be over. Once he became more familiar with his doctors, his disease, and his chances to survive, he began to think more about the future. But first he needed to tell the sports world what was wrong with him and how it would affect the rest of his life. He scheduled a news conference for the Monday following his operation. There, with his family, doctors, and members of his new team by his side, he announced that he had cancer and would not be racing until he beat it. And he stressed that he would beat it. "It's impossible to say when I'll be back racing, but I hold out hope to participate at the professional level in the 1997 season," he said. The directors of his new team also pledged their support.

When it was over, Lance went for his first chemotherapy treatment. Testicular-cancer chemo uses a mixture of drugs called BEP, which includes three highly toxic compounds called bleomycin, etoposide, and a platinum-based drug called cisplatin. The most important ingredient is the platinum, which has proved to be the most effective way to treat testicular cancer. Its use was pioneered at the Indiana University Medical Center in Indianapolis by Dr. Lawrence Einhorn. Until he discovered how to use it in treating testicular cancer, the disease was an almost certain death sentence. But Einhorn's very first patient was still cancer-free 20 years after the doctor had pioneered the treatment.

Lance was luckier than most cancer patients in one respect. His efforts to become a world-class cycling

A Cofidis cap covers Lance's bald head after chemotherapy treatments. Hair loss is one of the more benign side effects of chemo.

champ had made him almost impervious to pain. Although he would eventually have uncontrollable nausea, the first few weeks of chemo didn't affect much more than his appetite. However, like some cancer patients, Lance suddenly found himself in the middle of an insurance fiasco. His old team, Motorola, no longer existed, so his insurance coverage with the team had been canceled. The insurance carrier for his new team, Cofidis, claimed that the cancer was a preexisting condition and wouldn't cover the cost of the chemo. Lance suddenly found himself in an even worse predicament than he originally thought. Not only did he have cancer, but he now had no health insurance, no guarantee that he would ever ride a bike again, and no other way to make money. He was a high school graduate

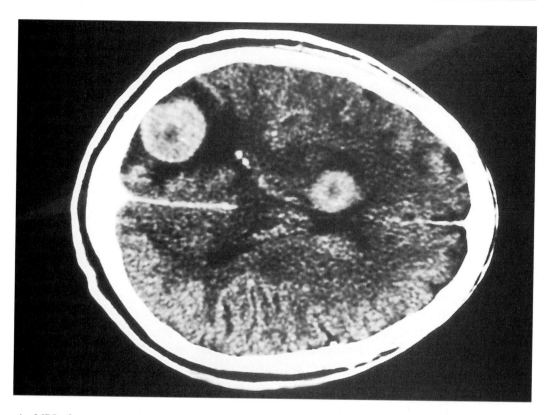

An MRI of a cancer patient's brain. The two dark spots are tumors. By the time Lance got treatment, his cancer had spread to his abdomen and lungs, and he'd developed two lesions on his brain.

who had never really had any other job except for being an athlete.

It was as if the cancer were purposely taking from him everything that had ever mattered. First, it kept him from racing and had threatened his ability to be a father. Then it had taken his strength as he suffered through chemo. Finally, it took him out of his financial comfort zone. Forced to sell his Porsche and other "toys," as he put it, Lance fell back on the lessons of self-reliance his mother had taught him as a child. Rather than becoming despondent, he became more determined than ever to make a comeback to professional cycling.

But cancer is a much stronger, more devious foe than any opponent Lance had ever faced. By what could only be called a stroke of luck, Lance received a letter from Dr. Steven Wolff of Vanderbilt University. Dr. Wolff's specialty was bone marrow transplants—a type of cancer treatment—but more importantly, he was a friend of Dr. Einhorn, the man who had pioneered the use of platinum in treating testicular cancer. At this time, Lance was receiving thousands and thousands of get-well cards and letters from his fans around the world. But he managed to open Dr. Wolff's letter, in which the doctor suggested that Lance go directly to Dr. Einhorn in Indiana. Dr. Wolff also wrote that he was a cyclist himself and would like to see Lance return to the sport. As usual, Lance jumped into action and called Dr. Wolff immediately. The result was a new ally in his fight against cancer.

The first thing Dr. Wolff did was convince Lance and his mother to seek more opinions from doctors in Houston and Indianapolis, which had the two best hospitals in the country for treating testicular cancer. With Dr. Wolff's help, Lance was able to set up consultations with the staff at the two hospitals. The closest one was in Houston, so he tried there first. What he found out was shocking. His blood count of HCG—a protein blood marker not found in healthy men, and a leading indicator of the cancer—was thousands of times higher than it should be. With his cancerous testicle removed, the only cancer should have been the golf-ball-sized spots on his lungs. But with a number that high, the Houston team suspected the cancer had spread, most likely to his brain.

Lance and his doctors in Austin quickly scheduled an MRI to scan his brain. Magnetic resonance imaging is a noninvasive procedure that produces computerized images of internal body tissue. The procedure required Lance to lay perfectly still in a tube not much bigger than his body. Many patients fear the MRI machine because they get claustrophobic, feeling as if they might suffocate. Lance was no different, but he was also fearing the results, which he already knew would be bad. Later, in Dr. Youman's office, Lance's deepest fears were confirmed. There were two spots on his brain where the cancer had spread.

The Indiana University Medical Center in Indianapolis is one of the country's top hospitals for the treatment of testicular cancer. On the advice of a doctor who had sent him a letter, Lance traveled here to explore his treatment options.

The next day Lance drove the three hours to Houston for his first face-to-face conversation with the doctors there. They were much more forceful than the doctors in Austin. The course of treatment recommended by the Houston doctors would leave Lance sterile and probably never able to race again. The drug bleomycin, which he was already taking, would be increased to wipe out the cancer, but it would also destroy his lungs. Next to legs of steel, large lung capacity is the cyclist's most important physical attribute. Being able to inhale and process vast amounts of oxygen is the only way for riders to conquer the climbs and sprints encountered in a race. And although Lance had said publicly that his main objective was simply to survive, he also wanted to pursue any treatment that might let him get back to the level of racing he was at before he became sick.

His gut feeling, echoed by his mother and friends, was that the Houston people were only interested in getting rid of the cancer; they had no regard for what his quality of life would be during the treatment or after it was over. One doctor in Houston even informed Lance, "Every day I'm going to kill you, then I'm going to bring you back to life." The doctor also told Lance in no uncertain terms that after the treatment he would be unable to walk, unable to have kids, and unable to ride his bike. The upside, of course, would be that he would be alive. But how does a man even begin to accept such harsh choices?

In the end, Lance's gut feeling was to seek yet another opinion, although he knew his time was running out. He had been told by more than one specialist that the cancer was spreading faster than had first been thought. But Lance needed to be sure that he had covered all the bases, had looked into every possible therapy, before settling on one. He and his friends had already scoured the Internet, downloading and printing out every bit of information they could find on testicular cancer and its treatments. Some were outlandish and crazy, some sounded good, and some were definitely legitimate. But none could give Lance what he wanted most: another chance to race in the Tour de France.

To make sure he was making the right decision, Lance called his friend Dr. Steven Wolff, the man who had told him about Dr. Lawrence Einhorn in Indiana. After describing what the doctors in Houston had told him, Lance asked Dr. Wolff what he should do. "It wouldn't hurt you to get one more opinion," said the doctor. So Lance called Dr. Einhorn's office at the Indiana University Medical Center in Indianapolis. Although Dr. Einhorn was out of the country at the time, his assistant, Dr. Craig Nichols, took Lance's call and told him to come to Indiana right away. Even though it was a Friday afternoon, he agreed to see Lance the next day. A few phone calls later Lance, his mother, and a few friends were at the Houston airport boarding a plane headed for Indianapolis.

Facing an uncertain future: After three surgeries and four chemotherapy cycles, Lance had to wait a year before he would know his long-range prognosis. If his cancer returned within that period, he would most likely die; if not, he was cured.

6

FIGHT OF
A LIFETIME

LANCE HAD MADE his reputation in the cycling community for being able to ride faster, farther, and harder than any of the other riders in the *peloton.* But the opponent he faced now seemed to be unstoppable. In the short space of a week Lance had learned that he had testicular cancer, had the affected testicle removed, started chemotherapy, and discovered that the cancer had moved into his brain. He had seen multiple doctors at various health-care facilities in southern Texas and had flown to Indiana to talk to even more doctors. He was tired, discouraged, scared, and reaching the end of his patience.

Lance and crew arrived in Indianapolis late on Friday afternoon. Early the next morning he was in a conference with Dr. Nichols, assistant to the man who had pioneered the treatment for testicular cancer, and a brain surgeon named Dr. Scott Shapiro, who would be reviewing scans of the lesions on Lance's brain. Lance's mother had faxed the details of his case to the doctors at the same time she had contacted the hospital in Houston, so they were familiar with what Lance was going through. The two experts took a look at Lance's X rays, blood counts, and the short history of his disease. Dr. Nichols was concerned yet confident. He admitted that Lance was in an advanced stage of the disease, but said that he had seen patients in worse situations who had survived. The spots on Lance's lungs—a dozen in all—were treatable with chemotherapy, which Lance already knew. But the two spots on his brain—both about the size of grapes—were a different matter. Chemo wouldn't work on brain cancer because a special membrane, called the blood-brain barrier, would keep the drugs from entering the brain. The usual treatment was radiation or surgery.

But first Dr. Nichols had some good news—at least compared with what Lance had heard in Houston. Unlike every other doctor Lance had seen, Dr. Nichols told Lance that although saving his life was priority one, there was a platinum-based protocol, or course of treatment, that could allow Lance to continue cycling. Whereas the Houston doctors wanted to step up the use of bleomycin in Lance's treatment—which would render his lungs unfit for competitive bicycle racing—Dr. Nichols was heading in the opposite direction. He wanted to remove bleomycin from the protocol entirely. Lance wasn't sure he had heard correctly at first, but Dr. Nichols assured him that it was a viable treatment that could cure him without some of the negative side effects of the bleomycin. Of course, it would affect him in other ways. The downside was an increase in the short-term discomfort: more nausea and weakness than the current treatment. But if the long-term result of the treatment was that it would allow him to return to competitive cycling, Lance was all for it.

The cancer on his brain was another problem altogether. Because chemotherapy wouldn't work for brain cancer, the only alternatives were radiation or surgery. Usually patients and their doctors choose radiation because of the inherent dangers of brain surgery. The problem with radiation, however, is that it can lead to vision and balance problems. Good vision and good balance are critical for a

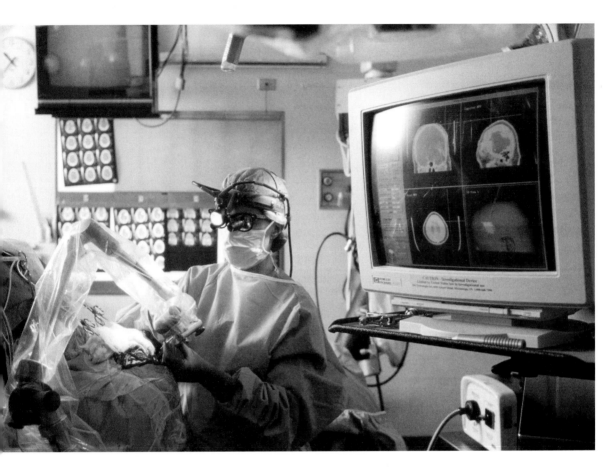

professional cyclist. The only choice for Lance was surgery, yet that brought its own list of things that could go wrong: seizures, paralysis, infection, hemorrhage. But that's why Dr. Shapiro was in on the initial consultation. After looking at the scans of Lance's brain lesions, Dr. Shapiro pronounced that it would be a rather routine operation. The good thing was that the tumors were on the surface of the brain and easily identified. He would be able to pinpoint their location, make small incisions, and remove them without too much damage to the brain tissue itself.

It was all up to Lance now. The doctors in Houston and in Indianapolis had presented their respective cases, and it was time to make a decision. As a professional cyclist,

Brain surgery (shown here) is generally a last resort; most cancer patients choose radiation treatments if possible. Because radiation can damage coordination and balance, however, Lance elected to undergo surgery, hoping that he might someday be able to return to bike racing.

Lance had been in this type of situation many times before. Was it the right time to make a jump and try to break from the group, or do you sit in with the guys for a few more kilometers? Do you go all out in the mountain stages, or do you wait until the time trial? Do you wait until you're completely healed, or do you risk reinjury while trying to come back soon? But never had he been faced with a decision as hard as the one he had to make on this day.

Fortunately he didn't have to make it alone. After having breakfast the next morning with his mother and the friends who had joined him in Indianapolis, Lance went back into the office of Dr. Nichols and told him he was ready for treatment. Dr. Nichols told Lance to come back on Monday morning to check in so he would be ready for surgery on Tuesday. A week after surgery Lance would begin his chemotherapy using the new platinum-based protocol called VIP, which includes the drugs vinblastine, etoposide, ifosfamide, and cisplatin. Dr. Nichols believed that this protocol would erase the cancer from Lance's body without damaging his lungs.

But first, of course, was the brain surgery. Even though Dr. Shapiro had seemed relaxed when discussing the lesions and the procedure, clearly it wasn't going to be a walk in the park. It was brain surgery, and no matter how routine or minor it seemed, it was the most dangerous medical procedure Lance would have to endure in his quest for a cure. The lesions were in accessible, though critical, areas of the brain. One was in a spot that affects vision, which was why things had been looking blurry to Lance just before his diagnosis. The other was near a part of the brain that affects coordination. Again, vision and balance are critical to a cyclist. To lose those would be to lose a whole way of life for Lance.

The night before the surgery, Lance wrestled with his own mortality for the first time. As with any major surgery, there was a possibility, however small, that Lance could die on the operating table. Yet not having the surgery would almost certainly lead to a quick, painful, and unnecessary death. Having been turned off from organized religion by his onetime stepfather, Terry Armstrong, who believed that boys needed to be beaten to make them behave (all the while proclaiming his own ardent belief in Christianity), Lance pondered what it would really mean if he were to die. Would he go to heaven or hell? And did it really matter? In his autobiography Lance claims that he came to the conclusion that although he didn't attend church regularly, he had always tried to be honest, to be loyal to friends, and to give something back to the community that had provided so much for him. When it came to a matter of belief or faith, Lance recognized that belief in God didn't necessarily come only from organized religion. He felt that to believe in the value of life was the important thing.

Confident that he was in good hands, and firm in his belief that everything would somehow turn out all right regardless of the outcome of the surgery, Lance submitted himself to an army of medical professionals on October 25, 1996. For six hours that day, Lance lay on the operating table, unaware of the passing of time. The skilled hands of Dr. Shapiro cut two small holes in Lance's skull, just millimeters from the cancerous spots. Then the doctor carefully scraped the damaged tissue from Lance's brain. One small slip and Lance's career, and very possibly his life, would be over. But Dr. Shapiro was an experienced surgeon with nerves of steel. The tissue was scraped without incident and was immediately examined by an attending pathologist—a doctor who specializes in identifying changes to various tissues brought about by disease. His job was to determine whether the tissue was cancerous, and, if so, how fast the cancer was spreading.

Finally it appeared as if Lance was getting a lucky break. The pathologist announced that the tissue was necrotic—dead. The cancer wasn't spreading in Lance's brain. This was the best news anyone connected with Lance had received in nearly a month. Lance, of course, was not aware of this new development. Hours later he woke up in a bed in the intensive care unit (ICU). His first thoughts were of his mother, his empty stomach, and the fact that he was still alive. Once the effects of the anesthesia had worn off completely, Lance would be ready for the next big battle in his fight against cancer: chemotherapy.

Cancer is a mysterious disease in many ways. Why some people get it while others do not still isn't completely understood, even by the doctors and other medical professionals who treat it on a daily basis. Certain substances have been linked to the different types of the disease, and lifestyle choices may also contribute. Lance didn't fit into any of the known high-risk categories. But no matter what type of cancer or what the ultimate cause of it may be, one thing is for sure: it's a terrible, painful, and, for most people, ultimately fatal disease.

Some people who have had the disease say that the only thing worse than having cancer is undergoing the treatment for it. The old saying "cut off one's nose to spite one's face" is an apt way to describe cancer treatment. As noted earlier, the radiation used to kill the cancerous cells also kills some healthy cells and can leave the patient permanently disabled. But the first step is often to surgically remove the affected area of the body. In Lance's case, his cancerous testicle was removed the day after the cancer was first diagnosed. Of course, this doesn't work too well when the affected body part is a vital organ, such as the lungs or the brain. Lance's cancer had spread to these parts also.

Chemotherapy is an alternative to radiation, but it has its own set of drawbacks. Basically, chemotherapy is the use of toxic drugs and chemicals that are slowly fed into the body via an intravenous line. (Also called an IV, an intravenous line is put directly into the patient's vein.) Normally these substances would be fatal, but they're given in carefully regulated doses that kill the cancer without killing the patient. Lance's doctors—Nichols and Einhorn—had already decided that the way to treat Lance was with a chemo protocol that would be harsh in the short term, but in the long run would preserve his lung capacity. Radiation was out of the question.

With the cancerous testicle and the brain lesions removed, the last big hurdle would be the spots of cancerous cells in Lance's lungs. It was now time for Lance to start his new chemotherapy sessions. He had already undergone one cycle of chemo in Austin, but with a different treatment protocol. At this point in his treatment his chance of being completely cured was pretty much a coin flip. Either the chemotherapy would work and he would live, or it wouldn't work and he would eventually die. But Lance and his doctors were optimistic, especially since his brain surgery had turned out so well.

Lance's chemo treatments went like this: five hours a day, for five straight days, he sat in a recliner in the hospital while the toxic chemicals dripped from an IV bag into his arm. The rest of the time he was either throwing up, in severe pain, or sleeping. After the fifth day, the chemo was discontinued for two weeks to allow Lance's body to recover. Then another chemo cycle would begin.

Lance dealt with the terrible side effects of the chemo—vomiting, painful urination, and so on—by telling himself he was purging the cancer from his body. He also relied on the support of his friends and family to get him through this difficult time. Although his mother eventually had to return to her job in Texas, Lance's longtime friend Jim Ochowicz, manager of the now defunct Motorola team, remained with Lance throughout the chemo.

Also helping to bolster Lance's spirits at this time was the support he was getting from his new team, Cofidis. His sponsors were also continuing to honor their contracts with him even though they could legally have gotten out of them. Nike, the international sportswear company, which had been one of Lance's sponsors since his days as a teenage triathlon champ, continued to support him in his sickness. But the biggest support he got at this time came from Oakley, the maker of high-quality eyewear. Not only did the company continue honoring its contract with Lance, it went so far as to force its insurance carrier to cover his medical expenses. Any financial worries Lance might have had were now over.

But the chemo treatments were making him sicker and sicker. When he first started them, Lance had scoffed at everyone's warning that he would soon be unable to eat or even walk. Sure, they made him feel bad, and his hair fell out, but for the first few cycles it wasn't any worse than the flu. As the weeks went on, however, he felt worse and worse. Unable to eat, and constantly vomiting from the nausea, Lance's once athletic body began to deteriorate. Fat, muscle, and bone mass began to suffer under the caustic burn of the chemotherapy. It ate at his teeth, his skin, and his blood. When he wasn't in Indiana undergoing the chemo, he was at home in Austin, hooked to an IV that was dripping more medicine into him—this batch to help protect his immune system from the harmful effects of the chemo.

From the time he was a toddler, Lance had been active: running, swimming, riding a bike, racing his car. He was constantly trying to keep moving. But the chemo had turned him into a completely different person. Used to spending hours a day riding a bike, he now could barely muster the strength to walk along the corridors of the hospital or down his driveway at home. Deep down inside, though, the tough, trash-talking, aggressive Texas Bull wouldn't let cancer or chemotherapy beat him down. He kept up an internal dialogue with his disease, telling it that it had picked the wrong guy to mess with. Just as he had done all his life, in this race against a fatal disease Lance put his head down and plowed ahead.

Lance finally began to receive good news: something was working. Whether it was the chemo alone or a combination of drugs and his bullheaded refusal to admit that he couldn't will himself back to health, Lance was slowly beating the disease. The blood protein markers that had been like a death sentence to him weeks earlier were getting lower with every passing day. Lance was feeling weak, and most days he had to struggle just to keep from passing out from the pain and nausea, but he was winning the battle against cancer.

Unfortunately, as time passed with Lance still far from a return to competition, Cofidis became nervous about his ability to return at all. The team sent a representative to the United States to visit Lance under the pretext of showing

Bill Stapleton, Lance's friend and agent (seen here with his client in happier times), worked hard to keep Lance under contract with Cofidis during his recovery. Ultimately, however, Lance would never race in a Cofidis uniform.

its unwavering support. When the reporters and TV cameras were present, the team representative stressed Cofidis's love and support of Lance. But in the back room, face-to-face with Lance's agent and friend, Bill Stapleton, there was another agenda. The team didn't want to fire Lance, but based on his current condition, it wanted to renegotiate his contract. Lance was being paid $2.5 million over two years, but he hadn't even had a chance to race in the Cofidis uniform. Although Stapleton argued that Lance was getting better and only looked so terrible because of the chemo, Cofidis could legally void the contract if Lance couldn't pass a physical administered by the team's doctor. Bill and Lance knew that Cofidis wasn't playing games, so they agreed to the new deal. Though still employed, Lance was making two-thirds of the money he had been making when he was first diagnosed.

Passing in and out of consciousness, Lance wasn't concerned with the dealings of Cofidis and his agent. Curled up on his bed and suffering from the effects of the chemotherapy, Lance's only concern was getting well.

There were two sides to Lance Armstrong's battle against his own body in the fall and winter of 1996–97. The biggest battle, of course, was just to live. Some days it didn't seem that he would survive—that if the cancer didn't get him, the chemotherapy would. But there were also days when, although weak, gaunt, and bald, Lance would think beyond mere survival. He constantly told the press and friends that racing again didn't matter, that what was important was simply getting well. But his actions spoke louder. Lance Armstrong was not out of the game just yet. Cancer and chemo might have double-teamed him, but he was going to come back, one way or another.

By mid-November, halfway through his chemo treatments, Lance had begun to show signs of his old competitive self. He even began taking short rides on his bike again with some friends. "I thought I was keeping up, but the truth was my friends were just being kind," he wrote in *It's Not About the Bike.* "In fact, they were moving so slowly they almost fell over sideways on their bikes. . . . I had little concept of how fast or slow we were going."

Lance even went so far as to enter a race near Austin—albeit on a purely ceremonial basis—to support cancer charities. He wanted to begin giving something back to those who had done so much for him. Besides the medical treatment he was receiving, countless letters of support from cancer survivors had reached him. He wanted to race again to show that cancer is not necessarily a killer.

By the end of December, after 12 weeks of chemotherapy, Lance's blood counts were almost back to normal and his chest X rays were beginning to show a real improvement. He wasn't out of the woods yet, but his chances of actually beating cancer were getting better with each passing day. His progress was so good, in fact, that his doctors agreed to allow him to begin light training. But regardless of how much Lance might have wanted to get back to racing, the cold, hard facts were that his body had taken a severe beating. "I really have no idea when I might be back in a real race," he said. "I don't want to race until I'm ready physically. Mentally, my motivation is there."

But all the motivation in the world won't win bike races, especially the Tour de France. From the time he launched his pro career, Lance's eye had been on the big prize: the yellow leader's jersey of the Tour. It had taken him four years to build up the technical skill and physical maturity to simply finish the Tour, to say nothing of making a serious run at actually winning it. But within a few short months the deadly combination of cancer and chemotherapy had eroded all of that hard-earned fitness. No matter how much he trained, it was highly doubtful that Lance would be ready to race in the 1997 season. While cycling fans the world over held their breath, and the cycling press printed speculation and rumor, Lance

Chemotherapy left Lance gaunt, weak, and unsure about whether he could return to competitive cycling.

was determined to take it one day at a time. "If you ask me what I hope for in the next year, he said, it's just to keep living."

After his last chemo treatment Lance returned to Austin. He was bald, weak, and scarred, but alive. The catheter that had been surgically implanted in his chest back in October was removed. Through this catheter the chemo drugs had been dripped into his body day after day, at three-week intervals. Having it removed was a signal to Lance that, possibly, he was cancer-free at last. But the disease doesn't work that way. It had sneaked up on him and progressed to an almost fatal level within days of being discovered, and it seemed to have retreated with just a few months of treatment. His doctors knew that it could come back just as quickly, just as severely, if he wasn't vigilant. His blood counts were still high, and there was still scar issue on his lungs, but Dr. Nichols was optimistic.

Lance was harder to convince. Though he was in what's called remission—meaning that at present he didn't have cancer—he still needed to be checked regularly for the disease. He had to have weekly blood tests and chest X rays, constant reminders of the cancer that had almost taken his life. Nonetheless, he was beginning to recover from the harsh chemo treatments. All throughout his treatment he had ridden his bike when he could, even if it was only a 30-minute trip around his neighborhood. Now that he was getting better, he was trying longer, harder rides, as well as taking time to enjoy his life.

Before the cancer, Lance's reason for riding a bike was all business. Being fast on a bike was what had gotten him out of Plano, bought him a big house on a lake in Austin, and taken him around Europe. He had never thought of it as being fun, or being something he truly loved to do. But not being able to ride had made it crystal clear to him that riding a bike was more to him than just another day at the office, so to speak. Lance came to the realization that he had lived a blessed, lucky life, and it all had nearly been taken away from him by cancer.

The old Lance might simply have jumped back on the bike immediately, determined to regain his lost fitness and return to racing as quickly as possible. But after having confronted his own mortality and, more important, shared his pain and suffering with other cancer patients, Lance decided to use his fame to help others with the disease. To that end, he started the Lance Armstrong Foundation, a charitable organization to help cancer patients and survivors of cancer. Headquartered in Austin, the foundation

An Austin resident shows her support for the city's favorite adopted son and his charitable organization. The Lance Armstrong Foundation grew out of Lance's desire to give back to the community that had stood by him during his struggle with cancer.

is supported by charitable donations, as well as the annual Ride for the Roses event. Following one of Lance's favorite training routes in the hills surrounding Austin, the Ride for the Roses takes place each spring and has attracted such cycling luminaries as Miguel Indurain and Eddy Merckx, as well as thousands of ordinary folks.

Starting the foundation was another way for Lance to give back to the community that had supported him during his illness. Although the purpose of the foundation was to help other people, an unforeseen benefit to Lance came about during the early planning stages of the foundation. One of the race's corporate sponsors had hired a local advertising and public relations firm to handle its contributions to the foundation. The account executive working on the campaign was a young woman named Kristin Richard. Known to her friends as Kik, she was not only beautiful but also outgoing and smart, and she had a no-nonsense attitude when it came to business. Her first encounter with Lance ended up in an argument over the phone about how her client was being treated by the foundation. But from such strained first impressions would eventually spring a deep-seated affection. Within a year, Kik would have a new name: Mrs. Lance Armstrong.

After starting the foundation, Lance turned his attention to the possibilities of racing again. He was still officially a member of the Cofidis team, but to keep his contract Lance would have to compete in four professional races in 1997. To test his fitness, Lance had started to go for training rides, some as long as four hours. But he was nowhere near being ready to race in the spring. His health had been wrecked by the chemo to such a degree that he was susceptible to colds, and he needed a long time to recover between rides. His doctors cautioned him to go slow, but Lance knew that no matter how careful he was, he wouldn't be able to race in 1997. Lance's brain was awash with questions: Was his career over? If Cofidis dropped him, would another team be willing to take a chance? Did he even care anymore?

Conquering hero: Lance, at the head of a line of riders, enters Paris, having overcome the field in the 1999 Tour de France—and late-stage testicular cancer.

7

VIVE LE LANCE!

FOR A LOT of athletes the story would end right here with "and they lived happily ever after." Simply beating cancer would be victory enough. But the competitive spirit in Lance Armstrong never let him rest on his laurels. Even during the most difficult days of chemotherapy, when all he really wanted was to live and not be sick, a voice deep inside Lance kept whispering about the possibility of racing again. By January of 1997 the cancer was in remission and Lance was beginning to feel a bit better. He had even begun weight training to build back some of the muscle lost to the chemo. Because he had started the treatment with almost no body fat, the chemo had attacked his muscles.

Although Lance was trying to increase his daily mileage on the bike, he quickly realized he would not be doing any racing in 1997. Instead he made plans to go to Europe as a tourist to offer support to his teammates from the sidelines rather than the front of the *peloton*. But even if Lance had felt up to racing, his doctors prohibited it until his cancer had been in remission for one full year. If he could remain cancer-free for one year, he could be declared cured. But if it came back, he was almost certain to die from it. Following his doctors' advice, Lance spent the spring and summer of 1997 in Europe, visiting the cities he had only ever raced in, hanging out with Kik, and regaining the strength and weight that he had lost to cancer.

But even as he was greeted with cheers by the European fans—especially the Italians, who still remembered his heartfelt tribute to their fallen countryman Fabio Casartelli—Lance was in danger of losing his place on the Cofidis team. His new contract called for him to race in four events during the 1997 season, but his doctors had forbidden him even to train hard for a year. Although it was a business decision, the news that he was being dropped by the team for failure to meet the obligations of his contract hit Lance hard. If it had happened while he was sick in the hospital, he might have accepted it, especially since the only thing he really cared about then was getting better. But to be on the road to recovery, to have conquered a disease as tough as cancer, only to be dropped from the roster was almost unbearable.

However, his reaction to the news, which came in September of 1997, revealed that a new, more confident and mature Lance was in control. Rather than throw a tantrum, Lance simply said, "They think I'm finished. That's great, I love that." He continued, "The perception is that once you get cancer, you're never the same afterward. I'd like to prove that wrong."

To do that, however, he would need a team. While there were many European teams that would still be happy to give him a job, none of them were willing to pay him more than the minimum salary, what first-year riders make. Lance was a former world champion, was a winner of two stages in the Tour de France, and had been ranked fifth in the world before his illness. He didn't want to work for a team that didn't really believe he could make a comeback. He would be getting the final word on his health in October, and every indication was that he would be ready to start racing again. But he needed a team to support him, to help him get back in shape and realize the one goal that had always been in the back of his mind: winning the Tour de France.

Lance's friend and agent, Bill Stapleton, was doing most of the legwork when it came to finding a new team. Lance did his part by appearing at the annual Interbike Trade Show in Anaheim, California, to promote his recovery and desire to return to racing. But it was Stapleton who had to fly all over the country and to Europe to meet with hard-nosed business executives to try to wrangle a deal for Lance. One of the most promising leads was the newly formed U.S. Postal Service team, which eventually signed Lance to a deal. Not only did the team meet Lance's salary demands, but he was excited to ride for an American-based team with ambitious plans to race in Europe and qualify for a spot in the Tour de France. The team's general manager was former Olympian Mark Gorski, who was determined to put together the best bike riders in America to take the European racing scene by storm.

No one, especially Lance, thought it was going to be easy. Still, because of his eternal optimism Lance may have underestimated the actual challenge of reviving his career. Working closely with his longtime coach Chris Carmichael, Lance began a schedule that had him in the weight room regularly and taking increasingly longer training rides. There were the good days, when Lance the cancer survivor would thrash his friends and teammates Frankie Andreu and Kevin Livingston. Then there were the bad days, when, catching a cold or feeling a little off, he would panic that the cancer was back. But with each passing day he grew stronger.

The combination of the cancer and the chemo had changed his body permanently. He had been a bulky, muscular 175 pounds of pure aggression. Now he was a thin, muscular 160 pounds of speed.

The first race in which Lance truly competed after his battle with cancer was the Ruta del Sol in Spain. He finished 14th. In the old days that would have been unacceptable. But considering that he had spent the previous year away from competitive cycling and undergone two surgeries plus chemotherapy, it was a clear sign that Lance Armstrong was back. Next on the schedule was another stage race called Paris-Nice in France. Spain in the spring is gentle and pleasant, with warm, sunny weather, but northern France in spring is another story. Cold, rainy, miserable, and gray, the weather is as much an opponent in this race as the other riders. The leader of the Postal Service team was George Hincapie, another young American with Tour de France aspirations. Lance was riding in the role of Hincapie's *domestique,* or support rider. His job was to help the leader by doing all the legwork: riding in front of him to break the wind, bringing him water or food, and waiting for him if he got a flat or crashed.

There aren't many racers who would be a support rider after having been a team leader, but Lance didn't mind. He knew he had a lot to prove, and if he were ever to take over as leader, he would need the trust and support of guys like Hincapie. Besides, they were old friends from the Motorola days. What Lance did mind was the freezing, wet weather that greeted the first stage of the race. Several hours into the stage, Hincapie got a flat. The team stopped to allow him to catch up, putting him more than 20 minutes behind the leader. The *domestiques'* job now was to push themselves to the breaking point to try to make up that time, allowing Hincapie to rest in their slipstream until he was back near the front. But Lance was having none of it. After a brief push he sat up from the aerodynamic racing position, pulled to the side of the road, and abandoned the race. It was too cold, too hard, and for some reason not where Lance wanted to be right at that moment.

Seeing Lance pull out of a race just because he didn't want to be there was a shocking development for his fam-

ily and friends. This was the man who used to seem impervious to pain and discomfort, who actually got stronger the harder and more unpleasant the race became. But cancer had changed Lance and his outlook. He didn't realize it at the time, but being a cancer survivor had made him reevaluate his past and his future. Taking a year off to recover and travel with Kik, to play golf, to eat the high-fat Mexican food he loved without worrying about his conditioning—experiencing simple pleasures like these, which he had denied himself in the past, made him question whether slogging through the freezing French rain was worth it.

Without telling his team or even his agent, Lance packed up and returned to Texas. Kik, who was living with

George Hincapie of the U.S. Postal Service team warms up before a time trial. During the 1998 racing season, Lance was supposed to be a support rider for Hincapie, but he abruptly dropped out of the Paris-Nice race and headed home to Austin.

*The Armstrongs at home.
Lance and Kristin "Kik"
Richard met through the
Lance Armstrong Foundation.*

him at this time, had quit her job and left family and friends to be in Europe while Lance raced. She also returned with him to Austin, but she was sure something wasn't right. This was not the Lance she knew.

Bill Stapleton, Jim Ochowicz, and Lance's mother believed that Lance just needed some time and the proper motivation to snap out of his funk. But as the weeks went by, the former world champion and America's best hope for winning the Tour de France turned into a channel-surfing, beer-swilling duffer more concerned with tee times than time trials. He hadn't even bothered unpacking his bicycle upon returning from Europe, so it sat in its box gathering dust in the garage.

Kik, like everyone around Lance, was concerned that he was wasting his talent and his fabulous second chance. But should they try to snap him out of his slump or just let him wallow for a while and hope he pulled out of it himself? The compromise was to give him his space but at the same time try to rekindle the fighting spirit of the old Lance. Finally Lance's coach, Chris Carmichael, convinced Lance that he needed either to have a formal press conference announcing his retirement, or to get off the couch and start racing.

Eventually, Lance agreed to compete in the U.S. Pro Championships, to be held in Philadelphia in June. Whether that would be the final high-level race of his career, he really didn't know. But with the Ride for the Roses, now the main fund-raiser for Lance's foundation, also coming up, it was time to get into shape anyway.

Carmichael believed that Lance would need an intensive 8-to-10-day training camp to be minimally fit even for the Ride for the Roses event. The two decided to rent a cabin in Boone, a little town high in the Appalachian Mountains of North Carolina, in April. And they decided to invite along Bob Roll.

Bob Roll was a longtime road racer who had become something of a cult figure on the cycling scene. Now 38 and a professional mountain-bike racer, Roll had been on the ground-breaking 7-Eleven team, the first U.S.-based professional cycling team to race in Europe. He was a fun-loving, storytelling bike freak who could make 100 miles in the mountains of North Carolina as pleasant as a walk in the park on a sunny spring morning.

Lance and Roll rode through the beautiful, isolated countryside in all kinds of weather, and the joy of being on a bike took hold of Lance's heart once again. As Roll related all his misadventures from the years he'd spent racing around the world, Lance realized that he too had stories about bad hotels, worse food, and the thrill and companionship of being part of a team of young

Americans trying to make a name for themselves on the back roads of Europe.

Near the rented cabin in Boone was Beech Mountain, where Lance had twice broken away from the field on his way to victory in the now defunct Tour DuPont. Toward the end of the training camp, Carmichael suggested riding the mountain. As they did, Lance was flooded with memories of past successes, and his competitive juices began to flow. Lance later wrote in his autobiography:

> As I started up the rise, I saw an eerie sight: the road still had my name painted on it.
>
> My wheels spun over the washed-out old yellow and white lettering. I glanced down between my feet. It said, faintly, *Viva Lance.*
>
> . . . As I continued upward, I saw my life as a whole. I saw the pattern and the privilege of it, and the purpose of it, too. It was simply this: I was meant for a long, hard climb.
>
> I approached the summit. Behind me, Chris could see in the attitude of my body on the bike that I was having a change of heart. Some weight, he sensed, was simply no longer there.
>
> Lightly, I reached the top of the mountain.
>
> . . . . I was restored. I was a bike racer again.

The month after the training camp, in May 1998, Lance experienced another joyful milestone. In a ceremony in Santa Barbara, California, he and Kristin Richard were married. They honeymooned for a couple days at a beach house in Santa Barbara, then returned to Austin for the Ride for the Roses.

In June, at the U.S. Pro Championships, Lance finished a respectable fourth in a race won by his friend and teammate George Hincapie. Then it was back to Europe, where Lance continued to improve, winning the Tour of Luxembourg and finishing fourth at the World Championships in the Netherlands. But the Tour de France wasn't on his schedule just yet.

It was a good thing, too, because the 1998 Tour was rocked by accusations of doping, and some of the best riders in the world were thrown out of the race for using illegal performance-enhancing drugs. The repercussions of that scandal-plagued Tour were felt throughout the rest of the year, and even into the beginning of the 1999 season. Riders such as Laurent Jalabert, the French star of the Spanish ONCE team, boycotted some of the spring races, including the always rainy Paris-Nice. Reporters worried about the effect the scandal would have on the upcoming Tour de France, and whether the sport would ever

Bicycling legend Bob Roll helped restore Lance's love of the sport during a training camp in the mountains of North Carolina.

be the same. Then, in the final stages of the Giro d'Italia— the Italian version of the Tour—just weeks before the Tour de France, the 1998 winner, Marco Pantani, was disqualified for using a banned substance. He was subsequently denied the right to compete in France.

During the winter off-season, Lance and his team had decided that 1999 would be the year for Lance to seal not only his comeback but his dominance of world cycling. It was an audacious decision, but one not made lightly. Ever since he turned pro back in 1992, Lance had been steadily building toward this conclusion. Cancer had set him back —indeed, it had nearly killed him. But the experience had also made him a better bike racer. Once called too heavy to be a climber, the new, lighter Lance was now a contender in the Alps and Pyrenees. Once headstrong and brash, the new Lance was thoughtful and strategic. Once easily discouraged, the new Lance had the patience born of tremendous suffering. Hard days in the mountains, killer sprints, soul-destroying time trials—what are these to a man who has beaten cancer?

On July 4, 1999, people in the United States were grilling burgers and shooting off fireworks to celebrate Independence Day. In France, American Lance Armstrong celebrated by winning the prologue time trial to start the 86th Tour de France in the race leader's yellow jersey. It wasn't really supposed to happen this way. Just a year before, Lance hadn't even been in good enough shape to compete in the race, much less have a chance of leading it. But even after his quick start in the 1999 Tour, no one thought he could actually stay in the lead. Many racers have won the opening time trial only to lose the lead and drop way back as the three-week race progresses. The director of the Postal Service team, Johan Brunyeel, even stated officially that his riders would not try to defend the yellow jersey in the flat stages but would concentrate on winning it back in the mountains later in the race.

The cycling fans and press of Europe were thrilled that Lance was in the leader's jersey. After all, he had fought his way back from what most thought to be a fatal disease, and what the French respect more than a winner is a competitor with courage and heart. Plus, Lance didn't have the taint of scandal that other racers had. No one, though, really thought he would win the whole thing—except Lance. But then in the second stage a freak accident caused the *peloton* to split in two. Lance was in the lead group and, realizing that some of his biggest rivals were caught behind the carnage, pushed the pace up a bit. He remained in yellow for another day.

The peloton in the mountains during the 1999 Tour de France. It was during the mountain stages that Lance, a much lighter rider since his bout with cancer, broke away from the field.

All things must end eventually, and by stage three, the
sprinters took over and Lance took a backseat to George
Hincapie, the star sprinter for the Postal team. Although
Hincapie didn't win a stage, he did his job by keeping the
team in the game while Lance waited for his chance to
attack. Meanwhile, ghosts of the previous year's drug
scandal still hovered about the Tour. Lance and three other
riders had tested positive for use of a steroid, but in
Lance's case the drug in his system had come from a
cream his doctor had prescribed for saddle sores, a common ailment of bike riders at all levels. Although Lance
was cleared of any wrongdoing, the rumors continued to
dog the race, especially in the French newspapers. The
rumor mill hit full stride after the individual time trial in
stage eight, when Lance completely demolished the
field—including the world time trial champion, Abraham
Olano—to regain the yellow jersey.

Stage nine saw the racers finally enter the Alps, where
the Tour could be won or lost in a single day. Lance had
never been great in the mountains, but on this day he was.
His new mastery of altitude was the result of his dramatic
weight loss, along with the intense training in the mountains of North Carolina and those near his adopted hometown of Nice, France, where he lived during the racing
season. As the days ticked by and Lance remained in the
lead, it became clear that not only had he conquered cancer, but he was about to conquer the world of professional
bicycle racing as well. While rumors continued circulating
in the press about drug use, Lance continued to test clean
and to proclaim his innocence. Although the French press
questioned his accomplishments, cycling fans were going
crazy. Even though Lance winning the Tour de France
would be like a French team winning the Super Bowl, true
cycling fans were celebrating his incredible spirit without
concerning themselves with nationality. The fact that
Lance had been on his deathbed just two years previous

made his story all the more popular with the people of France.

On July 25, 1999, a group of ragged, tired bicycle racers set out to ride the last stage of the 86th Tour de France. It began with some good-natured horseplay as the riders, tired beyond exhaustion, treated the beginning of the stage like a kind of carnival. As they approached Paris, however, things got more serious. Though Lance had wrapped up the overall victory, there was still a chance for a stage win, which could mean better contracts for the following year. But for Lance Armstrong the serious stuff was over. He didn't cross the finish line first that day, but he did cross it as the Tour's winner.

Lance and his U.S. Postal Service teammates were suddenly catapulted into the forefront of the sports world,

The Tour winner is rewarded with a kiss from his mother, Linda (right), and wife, Kik. Lance's inspiring comeback captured the imagination of people around the world.

Lance holds his infant son, Luke David Armstrong, on his shoulders after capturing his second straight Tour de France victory.

even in their home country, where bike racing isn't the near-obsession it is in Europe. Arriving back in the United States, they did a whirlwind tour of the morning talk shows and spoke with the president. Lance told one interviewer, "I'm prouder of being a cancer survivor than I am of winning the Tour de France. Believe me."

Just as he was a cancer survivor, so too was he a bike racer. There was no way for him to separate that part of himself from the part that had beaten the terrible disease. His victory in the 1999 Tour de France was one of the most miraculous sports stories of the 20th century—and his victory in the 2000 Tour became the biggest sports story at the start of the 21st century. There were those who had said that he couldn't do it again, that he'd won the first time only because of lucky breaks and because racers like Italy's Marco Pantani and Germany's Jan Ulrich weren't in the 1999 race. Well, they were in the 2000 Tour, and Lance whipped them pretty convincingly, making the famed climber Pantani suffer in the Alps like no one had ever done before. Following the Tour, Lance joined the U.S. Olympic team in Sydney, Australia, where he finally won the elusive Olympic medal. He'd been hoping for years to bring home the gold, but he had to settle for a bronze in the individual time trial—losing the gold to his current teammate and old Tour DuPont rival Viatcheslav Ekimov, and the silver to Tour de France rival Jan Ulrich.

Armstrong came back strong in 2001 to win his third consecutive Tour de France as well as the Tour of Switzerland. In the 2001 Tour de France, with many top competitors riddled with injuries, Armstrong's toughest challenger was Jan Ullrich. In 2002, Lance went on to win his fourth straight Tour de France victory. The win places him just one victory away from the current record of five straight Tour de France wins.

But the real postcancer victories for Lance are the births of his children. His son, Luke David Armstrong, was born on October 12, 1999, and his twin daughters, Isabelle Rose and Grace Elizabeth, were born on November 20, 2001. For all his momentous victories in bike races and his spectacular recovery from late-stage testicular cancer, the one and only thing that really matters now to Lance is to be the kind of father he never had.

CHRONOLOGY

1971   Lance Armstrong born on September 18, 1971

1984   Wins IronKids Triathlon

1987   Competes in triathlons as a professional

1990   Travels to Moscow to compete in the 1990 Junior World Championships of bicycle racing

1991   U.S. junior national champion

1992   Finishes 14th in the road race at the Olympics in Barcelona, Spain; turns professional immediately after the Olympics; finishes last in the San Sebastián Classic, his first race as a pro

1993   Wins U.S. Pro Championships; beats Europe's top riders at the World Championships in Oslo, Norway; finishes second in the Tour DuPont; wins a stage in his first Tour de France but drops out of the race before the finish

1994   Second-place finishes in the Tour DuPont and the Liège-Bastogne-Liège; wins Thrift Drug Classic; starts but does not finish the Tour de France

1995   Wins the Tour DuPont, his first stage-race victory; finishes Tour de France with one stage win; wins San Sebastián Classic

1996   Wins Tour DuPont, Fleche Wallone; drops out of Tour de France because of a cold; finishes 12th in the Olympic road race in Atlanta; diagnosed on October 2 with advanced testicular cancer; undergoes operations to remove the affected testicle, lesions on his brain; begins chemotherapy

1997   Starts Lance Armstrong Foundation; meets Kristin "Kik" Richard; signs contract with the U.S. Postal Service racing team after being dropped by Cofidis

1998   Marries Kik Richard and returns to bike racing; wins Tour of Luxembourg, Sprint 56K Criterium, Cascade Classic, Rheinland Pfafz Rundfahrt; second place at First Union International

1999   Wins Tour de France; son Luke David Armstrong born on October 12

2000   Successfully defends Tour de France title; bronze medal in time trial at the Olympic Games in Sydney, Australia

2001   Wins third straight Tour de France; wins Tour of Switzerland; twin daughters, Isabelle Rose and Grace Elizabeth, born on November 20th

2002   Wins fourth consecutive Tour de France; second in Criterium International

FURTHER READING

Abt, Samuel. *Lance Armstrong's Comeback from Cancer: A Scrapbook of the Tour de France Winner's Dramatic Career.* San Francisco: Van der Plas Publications, 2000.

Armstrong, Kristin. *Lance Armstrong: The Race of His Life.* New York: Platt & Munck, 2000.

Armstrong, Lance, with Sally Jenkins. *It's Not About the Bike: My Journey Back to Life.* New York: G. P. Putnam's Sons, 2000.

Armstrong, Lance; Chris Carmichael; and Peter Nye. *The Lance Armstrong Performance Program: The Training, Strengthening, and Eating Plan Behind the World's Greatest Cycling Victory.* Emmaus, Pa.: Rodale, 2000.

Stewart, Mark. *Sweet Victory: Lance Armstrong's Incredible Journey.* New York: Millbrook Press, 2000.

Wilcockson, John, and Charles Pelkey. *Lance Armstrong and the 1999 Tour de France.* Boulder, Colo.: Velo Press, 1999.

WEBSITES

Lance Armstrong Foundation
www.laf.org./

Lance Armstrong On-line!
www.lancearmstrong.com/

APPENDIX

FURTHER INFORMATION AND RESOURCES

American Cancer Society (ACS)
For more information on all types of cancer and the services of the ACS, call 1-800-ACS-2345 or e-mail from the ACS website, www.cancer.org. Follow links for specific information on testicular cancer or go directly to: www3.cancer.org/cancerinfo/load_cont.asp?ct=41&language=English

National Cancer Institute (NCI)
The NCI has prepared a booklet to help patients and their families better understand and deal with testicular cancer. For more information, call 1-800-4-CANCER (1-800-422-6237) or visit the website at: rex.nci.nih.gov/WTNK_PUBS/testicular/index.htm

INDEX

PICTURE CREDITS

JOHN THOMPSON is a current contributor to, and former editor of, *Mountain Bike* and *Bicycling* magazines. He lives in Breckenridge, Texas, where he grew up. In his spare time he rides his bike, listens to opera, and feeds his cat.

JAMES SCOTT BRADY serves on the board of trustees with the Center to Prevent Handgun Violence and is the vice chairman of the Brain Injury Foundation. Mr. Brady served as assistant to the president and White House press secretary under President Ronald Reagan. He was severely injured in an assassination attempt on the president, but remained the White House press secretary until the end of the administration. Since leaving the White House, Mr. Brady has lobbied for stronger gun laws. In November 1993, President Bill Clinton signed the Brady Bill, a national law requiring a waiting period on handgun purchases and a background check on buyers.